Sitting with Death:

Buddhist Insights to Help You Face Your Fears and Live a Peaceful Life

Margaret Meloni, PhD

Sitting With Death: Buddhist Insights to Help You Face Your Fears and Live a Peaceful Life Copyright ©2021 Margaret Meloni

All rights reserved. No part of this publication may be reproduced, distributed, or transmitted in any form or by any means, including photocopying, recording, or other electronic or mechanical methods, without the prior written permission of the publisher, except in the case of brief quotations embodied in reviews and certain other non-commercial uses permitted by copyright law.

To contact the author, visit www.margaretmeloni.com.

ISBN: 978-1-953596-20-8 (paperback)

ISBN: 978-1-953596-21-5 (ebook)

Library of Congress Number: 2 0 2 1 9 1 6 8 5 2

Cover Design by Eric Labacz

The Publishing Portal
www.thepublishingportal.com
Los Angeles, California

Printed in the United States of America

Praise for *Sitting with Death*

Reading Margaret's tender, wise book feels like sitting with your best friend! Margaret shares wisdom from twelve Buddhist teachers whose guidance helps us (and her) meet death and dying with less fear and find the gifts of comfort and joy hidden within grief and loss. With her big heart of compassion, cracked open by the deaths of her husband, father and mother, Margaret encourages us to use death as a life coach. I'm touched by her unfailing commitment to kind understanding and love in the face of our ultimate destiny.

—Trudy Goodman, PhD, Founder, InsightLA

In her book, *Sitting with Death*, Margaret Meloni invites the reader into a conversation with twelve Buddhist meditation teachers on the many faces of death. She intermingles passages from Buddhist scripture with insights from experienced contemplative practitioners, active in the field of death and dying. It was refreshing to hear not only these teachers' wisdom offerings, but their personal stories as well. This gives her book an approachable, deeply human and intimate quality. *Sitting with Death* is filled with practical advice on the many challenges of facing death or working with the dying. It is also a great introduction to Buddhist teachings on impermanence and their secular application in contemporary society.

—Judith L Lief, author of *Making Friends with Death: A Buddhist Guide to Encountering Mortality* (judylief.com)

Dedication

Dedicated to the frontline workers of the COVID pandemic.

Dedicated to all paid and unpaid caregivers.

Dedicated to those who accompany us to the gates of death...family members, healthcare workers, hospice teams, funeral home and graveyard staff.

May we follow your example in generosity and service.

May we emulate your courage and sacrifice when it is our turn to serve you.

~ As suggested by Holly Hisamoto

To all beings, may you be well, may you be happy, may you be at ease, and may you be free from suffering.

Acknowledgments

Years ago, one of my professors told me, "The right people show up." Because this was in a leadership course, and because he was discussing public speaking, I took him very literally. He was reassuring us that when we stand up to speak, it does not matter how many people are in the room. It was about who was in the room. They were the right people. Later, I began to see how "The right people show up," was about so much more than who comes to your class or seminar. In life, the right people show up. They show up so that we can be of service to one another on our path. In writing this book the right people showed up, and I am grateful for their generosity, wisdom, and compassion.

Noël Alumit, Timber Hawkeye, Holly Hisamoto, Venerable De Hong, Cayce Howe, Seth Zulho Segall, Dave Smith, Mary Stancavage, Venerable Sumitta, Venerable Karma Lekshe Tsomo, Diane Wilde, and Venerable Guan Zhen; when I asked you if you would speak to me about your experiences with death and grief and Buddhism, you all showed up. You are my twelve wise teachers, and it is with your support and insight that I am able to share this book, so that all may benefit from teachings around Death Dhamma.

And you, dear reader—here you are. You too are the right person, showing up. Ready, willing, and able to face your fears, make friends with death, and live your life with peace and strength. And I hope – to help others do the same.

Life is swept along,
next-to-nothing its span.
For one swept to old age
no shelters exist.
Perceiving this danger in death,
one should drop the world's bait
and look for peace. (SN 2.19)

The Joy of Death

How can something be both happy and sad? How is it that in this moment, and the moments to come you can feel joy and then pain? Relief and then grief?

Death can be difficult, tricky, and capricious. For the ill, the tired, the ones who cannot come back, death is a welcome escort. Here to bring yourself or someone you love to a place of peace. Other times death appears, unbidden, unwanted but still simply acting as an escort.

What is there for you to do when you are left behind? Just breathe. Let the tears come.

Breathe in and know that there is sadness. Breathe out and know that there is joy. Breathe in, breathe out and know that death is life.

Sitting with Death:

Buddhist Insights to Help You

Face Your Fears and Live a

Peaceful Life

Table of Contents

Introduction .... *xv*

Chapter 1
Introducing Our Twelve Wise Teachers 1

Chapter 2
Learning About Death 7
Easing In Versus Jumping In *7*
Death: Front and Center *9*
The Gift of Acceptance *10*
On Processing Death *12*
Monks and Nuns Learn About Death Too *13*

Chapter 3
Training for Death 19
The Five Recollections *20*
On Helping Others *22*
Do You Have a Training Plan? *25*
Training Level One: Impermanence *27*
Training Level Two: Keep Death in Mind *27*
Training Level Three: Practice the Five Recollections ... *28*
Training Level Four: Meditate on Death *29*

Chapter 4
Death Has Many Faces 31
Euthanasia and Suicide *32*
Losing Our Parents *34*
Death and Privilege *36*
Dying Alone *40*
Try to Bring Peace *42*

Chapter 5
Grief Has Many Faces Too 45
Buddhism Is Not a Silver Bullet *47*
Describable and Indescribable *49*
On Where You Grieve *52*
On Meditating *53*
On Being Prepared *55*

Chapter 6
This Is Not Easy for Any of Us 61
Overcoming Regret *62*
Have an Open Heart *64*

Chapter 7
Impermanence and Attachment **67**
   On Love and Attachment *68*
   Impermanence Is Fun (No Really) *69*
   No Blame, No Shame *71*
   Let's Keep Learning *72*

Chapter 8
Grief Has No Schedule **75**

Chapter 9
Talking to Dead People **79**
   Wonderful and Unexplainable *79*
   Finding Joy *80*
   The Case of the Lemon Cupcakes *81*
   May Your Merit Find Them *83*
   You Have a Team *84*
   It's Not About Clinging *85*

Chapter 10
It's Not About Cutting Off Feelings **87**
   Just Be Happy *88*
   You Are Not Your Emotions *90*
   All Feelings Are Welcome *91*

Chapter 11
Accepting Sadness and Joy **95**
   Today I Will Be Happy and Sad and *96*
   Hello, Come Sit with Me *97*

Chapter 12
Don't Let Fear Stop You **99**
   Develop a Mind Filled with Compassion *100*
   Give the Gift of Peace *101*
   Proceed with Curiosity *103*
   No, You Stop! *104*
   Suffering to End Suffering *105*

Chapter 13
Death Practices **109**
   Find Your Balance *113*
   Live in Peace, Die in Peace *114*
   Strength Training Requires Strong Teaching *116*

Chapter 14
How to Help Yourself 119
    Be Your Own Best Friend 119
    Gratitude and Acceptance 121
    Back to the Basics 122
    Contemplating Death 125
    Consistency Is Key 126

Chapter 15
Death Dhamma *Ahas* 129
    Other Cultures Can Teach You About Death 129
    Each Death Reveals Something New 131
    Death Can Be Joyful 132
    Grief Brings Gifts 135
    You Can Become a Gift to Others 137

Conclusion 139

Resources 143
    Books 143
    Courses 144
    Podcasts 144
    Websites— People 145
    Websites—Teachings 145

About the Author 147

Abbreviations

These are the abbreviations used for the Pāli Buddhist texts, which are quoted throughout this book.

AN	*Aṅguttara Nikāya*
Dhp	*Dhammapada*
DN	*Dīgha Nikāya*
Iti	*Itivuttaka*
Khp	*Khuddakapātha*
MN	*Majjhima Nikāya*
SN	*Saṃyutta Nikāya*
Sn	*Sutta Nipāta*
Thag	*Theragāthā*
Ud	*Udāna*

Introduction

Carpooling with Death: How Living with Death Will Make You Stronger, Wiser and Fearless was about my own journey to make friends with death, and to recount a time in my life when I was tempted to think that death had been stalking me. I had developed a fear of death. Not *my* death, but the death of the people and animals I loved. I became conscious of the fact that we would all die, and that meant that the day would come when I would have to say goodbye to the people I loved the most. As I came to realize that death was unavoidable, I made friends with the Grim Reaper. I even considered getting in the carpool lane with him as my passenger. I am still here, so you know he was not coming for me. But he did pick up my father, and then two years later, he returned for my mother and my husband. And after these and some other visits, I learned that Grim—his friends call him Grim—is not a bad guy. Being a Buddhist helped me to accept that the Grim Reaper was just doing his job.

My primary purpose in sharing my journey was to help others. To shine a light on the fact that there is much discomfort around death. When you go through the loss of your loved ones, it is going to be a wild ride. But you are not alone. This was a story that was inside me, needing to get out. And I hoped that it would help others makes sense out of losing their loved ones, the complicated emotions that show up, and all the crazy human behaviors that surface too. The process of writing my story helped me to reconcile life and death and how Buddhism gave me the strength I needed. In fact, as many of my mentors have told me, it probably helped me the most. There is a Zen expression, "The teacher teaches what he most needs to learn." True enough.

After living and sharing my story, I began to wonder, *what is this like for others*? Specifically, what is this like for other Buddhists, and do Buddhist spiritual teachers have the magic "no suffering" wand? And perhaps if I wondered, others would too? And so the quest began. I sought out Buddhist spiritual teachers and invited them to discuss death with me. To share their experiences with death, and to teach me what has been the most useful to them as they dealt with death and grief. Twelve wonderful wise teachers answered my call to help me learn more about how to deepen my friendship with death. And in doing so, they reached out to you. Because here you are, bringing curiosity and an open heart, so that you can train for the death of your loved ones. You can decide how to include death in your own practice. And as a result, you will live more fully, with more compassion for others, and more peace for yourself.

The ability to naturally be comfortable with death is rare. However, it is a life skill that you can develop, and as with other skills, your level of accomplishment will fluctuate. Beginner, Advanced Beginner, Intermediate—think of it in a way that makes sense to you. And know that these are not competitive skills, they are coping skills. You have a working knowledge of the Four Noble Truths, the Noble Eightfold Path, and impermanence. You are ready to use Buddhist teachings to strengthen your skills. Our twelve wise teachers are here, in this book, waiting for you and seeking to show you their versions of Death Dhamma.

Chapter 1

Introducing Our Twelve Wise Teachers

How do I know what other Buddhists think about death and grief? Where did the wisdom and compassionate sharing for this book originate? From our twelve wise teachers. Once I realized that others would want to learn from the experiences of Buddhist spiritual teachers, I reached out. Some of our teachers I knew, some I did not. What I quickly learned was that those who understood the importance of training for death, answered me quickly and decisively. Here are the twelve, who unselfishly and compassionately shared their thoughts and experiences, so that we all might benefit, and so that we all might lead a peaceful life—a life that leads to a peaceful death.

Noël Alumit—Noël is an actor, *Los Angeles Times* best-selling author, and Buddhist Pastor. He is a recipient of a 2020–21 City of Los Angeles (COLA) Individual Artists Fellowship. He received his BFA in acting from USC, and his MDiv in Buddhist Chaplaincy from University of the West. Visit Noël at *noelalumit.com*.

Timber Hawkeye—Timber is the best-selling author of *Buddhist Boot Camp* and *Faithfully Religionless*. His books and the *Buddhist Boot Camp* podcast offer a secular and nonsectarian approach to being at peace with the world (both within and around us), with the intention to awaken, enlighten, enrich, and inspire. *BuddhistBootCamp.com*

Holly Hisamoto—Holly (she/her/hers) is an academic advisor, providing support and education to university students in exploratory phases of life and career decision-making. Holly was previously a Buddhist chaplain in health care for eight years, serving hospice, pediatric, and emergency care settings. Holly has a BA in Religious Studies from Naropa University in Boulder, Colorado, and an MDiv in Buddhist Chaplaincy from University of the West in Rosemead, California. A ngakmo, or lay Buddhist priest, Holly's priority, regardless of professional role, is to support persons and communities to find pathways out of suffering. This often includes talking about death and dying, anti-racism education, peer support for trauma-informed caregivers, enjoying interfaith and cross-cultural friendships, and engaging an ongoing dialectic between social action and contemplative practice.

Introducing Our Twelve Wise Teachers

Venerable De Hong—Venerable De has been a Buddhist monk since 2006 in the Vietnamese and Chinese Pure Land Tradition. He was also ordained in the Burmese's Theravāda Tradition of the Mahasi Lineage in 2014. Venerable De is one of the cofounders of the Engaged Buddhist Alliance (EBA) and has volunteered in several state prisons in California, teaching mindfulness meditation and Buddhist psychology since 2013. He's also in charge of EBA's correspondence courses for incarcerated students in other remote California state prisons as well as in Washington and Arizona.

engagedbuddhistalliance.org

Cayce Howe—Cayce is a Senior Meditation/Dharma teacher for InsightLA and teaches meditation at mental health facilities in Southern California. He is cofounder of the *More Happiness Less Suffering* Podcast alongside Dr. Monisha Vasa, and author of the dharma poetry book *Becoming Water: Heart Path to Wisdom*. Learn more about Cayce by visiting *www.caycehowe.com*.

Seth Zulho Segall, PhD—Seth is a clinical psychologist and Zen Buddhist priest who taught on the faculties of four universities, including twenty-eight years on the clinical faculty of the Yale University School of Medicine. He is a former Director of Psychology at Waterbury Hospital, a former President of the New England Society for the Study of Trauma and Dissociation, and a former chaplain associate at White Plains Hospital. He is currently the science writer for the *Mindfulness Research Monthly*. Dr. Segall's books include *Buddhism and Human Flourishing* (Palgrave MacMillan, 2020), *Living Zen: A Practical Guide of a Balanced Existence* (Rockridge, 2020), and *Encountering Buddhism: Western Psychology and Buddhist Teachings* (SUNY Press, 2003). He maintains a blog on Buddhist topics called *The Existential Buddhist* at *www.existentialbuddhist.com*

Dave Smith—Dave is an internationally recognized Buddhist meditation teacher, addiction treatment specialist, and published author. His background is rooted in the Insight Meditation tradition, and he was empowered to teach through the Against the Stream Buddhist Meditation Society. He has extensive experience bringing meditative interventions into jails, prisons, youth detention centers, and addiction treatment facilities. Dave teaches residential meditation retreats and classes, provides training and consulting in both secular and Buddhist contexts, and works with students through his meditation mentoring program. He is the founder of the Secular Dharma Foundation. Visit Dave at *www.davesmithdharma.com*.

Mary Stancavage—Mary has practiced meditation and yoga, and has cultivated a spiritual practice for over thirty years. In 2009, she was empowered to teach Buddhadharma. She teaches classes and retreats, coaches and mentors individuals, and has facilitated several *A Year to Live* groups over the years. She has served as a volunteer hospital chaplain and been involved with leadership in several nonprofit

Introducing Our Twelve Wise Teachers

organizations over the years both in meditation and in the social justice arena. For the last several years, Mary has investigated what it means to live with an undefended heart. For more information, visit *marystancavage.org*. Fun fact: Mary spent several seasons working as an archaeologist in Syria.

Venerable Sumitta—Venerable Sumitta is currently a PhD Research scholar at the University of the West, and is pursuing his research thesis on "Philosophy of Arahanta Ideal as Depicted in Mahaniddesa." He has worked as an adjunct faculty at the University of the West, teaching Fundamentals of Buddhism and Introduction to Buddhist Psychology. He is actively engaged in social welfare and spiritual care activities in California by conducting Dhamma Talks, meditations, and Pāli language teaching. He is the founder of "Dhamma USA" (*dhammausa.org*), a community-based charity organization to launch his social welfare and spiritual care activities. He works as a prison care volunteer for Engaged Buddhist Alliance in Southern California.

Venerable Karma Lekshe Tsomo—Venerable Karma is a Buddhist nun, scholar, and social activist. She is a professor at the University of San Diego, where she teaches Buddhism and World Religions. She is cofounder of the Sakyadhita International Association of Buddhist Women (*sakyadhita.org*), and the founding director of the Jamyang Foundation, which supports the education of women and girls in the Himalayan region and the Chittagong Hill Tracts of Bangladesh. She took novice precepts as a Buddhist nun in France in 1977 and full ordination in Korea in 1982. Her most recent books include *Women in*

Buddhist Traditions (New York University Press, 2020), and *Buddhist Feminism and Femininities* (SUNY Press, 2019).

Diane Wilde—Diane has studied meditation in various traditions since 1990. In 2001, she was a founding member of Sacramento Insight Meditation (SIM). She founded Buddhist Pathways Prison Project (aka Boundless Freedom Project) in 2010, and has been a prison chaplain for eighteen years. She is a graduate of Sati Center's Buddhist Chaplaincy program, and graduated from Spirit Rock Meditation Center's Community Dharma Leadership Training Program. She is a board member of Sati Center for Buddhist Studies at the Sacramento Dharma Center. In 2015, she was lay-ordained as a Buddhist minister by Gil Fronsdal. To listen to some of Diane's previously recorded talks, visit SIM's audio dharma library at *sactoinsight.org/tag/diane-wilde*.

Venerable Guan Zhen—Venerable Guan Zhen is a Buddhist monk in the Chinese Chan tradition. He has been a monk for more than twenty years. He came to the United States to pursue his education. He currently holds an MDiv in Buddhist Chaplaincy and a master's degree in social work. From 2012 thru 2014, he served as a chaplain candidate in the United States Army Reserves. His current focus is on hospital work, and he recently completed his four units of CPE residency at Stanford Health Care, providing spiritual care to the terminally ill and their families. He considers it an honor when families from all religious backgrounds entrust him with their spiritual care.

Chapter 2

Learning About Death

Do you remember how you first learned about death? Our ability to process death begins with how we are introduced to it. We learn from our first encounters, and we learn by watching our elders. Some of us are given gradual lessons. First, the death of a pet, then perhaps a grandparent, then other senior friends or family members, maybe an aunt or uncle.

Like many of us, Cayce Howe went through this type of a progression in his life.

Easing In Versus Jumping In

When he was in the seventh grade, Cayce's first dog, Shadow, died. At that point in his life, all of Cayce's memories included Shadow. He recalls his mother being on the phone with the veterinarian. After the phone call, she turned to Cayce and she told him that Shadow had just passed away. He had heard of death, but this was his first direct experience—this was real. He knew that Shadow was never coming back. This was not a classmate losing their cat or hearing that someone's grandparent died. This was *his* dog. And Shadow was like a family member.

It was crushing. Cayce remembers being in shambles. Shadow's absence was unbearable to contemplate. As difficult as it was, Cayce knows that this was an excellent introduction to death, grief, and the rising and falling of feelings.

Like Cayce, my first experience with death was also with a beloved dog. Bonnie Muffin Speckleberry was our dog, a cute little Maltese puppy who was not even a year old. Her name was originally just Bonnie. For some reason, I felt this was incomplete. If I had a first name, a middle name, and a last name, then so should our dog. Bonnie had just come home from the veterinarian's office, with a clean bill of health, but she was not OK. Soon my parents would have to make the difficult decision to have her put down. I remember crying myself to sleep.

Our twelve wise teachers all shared their introduction to death with me. While some are similar, no two are the same. I bet that your story has common threads with others, and yet is still uniquely yours. Let's start our exploration of how others have experienced death with some of their introduction-to-death stories.

While Cayce and I may have had the opportunity to ease into death, Noël Alumit jumped in with both feet. In the early 1990s, when there was no known cure for AIDS, Noël volunteered at a hospice that was primarily filled with AIDS patients. Talk about an intense introduction to death! He was on the front line, holding people's hands as they died, witnessing too many people dying without contact from their families, and, as he later realized, seeing more death than he was able to process.

You might call Holly Hisamoto's introduction to death traditional with a twist. Growing up in Alaska, Holly saw death as a normal result of hunting and fishing. She knew that when her father would go hunting or fishing, he was bringing back animals who had started the day off alive. It was very much a circle-of-life type of existence. Not all the animal deaths that she observed were the result of hunting or fishing, some were a more natural effect of the life cycles of animals living in the wild. When she was six years old, she learned that death did not just happen to Alaskan wildlife. Her favorite aunt died by suicide, and that was a very different introduction to death. Holly uses the phrase *death comes crashing in*. When her aunt died, death came crashing into the bubble that Holly inhabited. Animal deaths were one thing, but until this point, human life had continuity. Her aunt's death was very real and very visceral.

When Holly received the news of her aunt's death, almost immediately her body felt cold. She experienced strong feelings of disbelief and was unable to wrap her mind around the fact that her aunt was dead. She hid in her room, crying into her pillow. Her sorrow expressed itself in a very physical way. Now, Holly recognizes that she was in shock.

Death: Front and Center

Timber Hawkeye likes to say that at an early age, death was front and center for him. I suspect this is why he did not shy away from discussing death with me. I knew him through his website, Buddhist Boot Camp (*www.buddhistbootcamp.com*). He had such an interesting background—he was born Jewish, ordained Buddhist, uses a Hindu mantra, and his morning meditation is a Catholic prayer. I recall thinking, "Now this is a person who is going to have an interesting perspective." And he does.

Timber's family never shied away from discussing death. He appreciates that his family was open to discussing difficult topics. Timber grew up in Israel during a time when every morning the newspaper would list how many Israeli soldiers had been killed the day before. Watching his mother cry for the dead soldiers and their families was part of his daily routine.

This is how it was, every morning. Finally, one day, young Timber asked his mother, "Did you know them?" And she said no. To which he replied, "Well, then can we speed this up, because I still have to get to school." His intention was not to be uncaring. He had learned that every day there would be death, but he and his family were still alive, and they needed to continue with the process of living.

Early deaths are not always pets and wild animals or soldiers whose names you only know from the news. Diane Wilde considers herself fortunate that she had a very real experience with death when she was eight years old. Her dear friend, who was just seven, died of a heart condition. The community was shaken to its core. None of her young friends wanted to go to the funeral. Their parents did not want to go either. It was horrible. Diane looks back at her eight-year-old self and remembers that she felt bad for his family. Diane also wanted to see her friend one last time, to say goodbye to him. So down the street she went to visit the family. There was her friend, Joey, in a child's casket, wearing a white suit, and holding rosary beads. Joey's parents were so appreciative that Diane came to say goodbye. They could not stop hugging her, and they thanked her profusely. It was the best thing that she could have done. Seeing Joey looking so beautiful and peaceful helped Diane let go of her fear of death. Diane is one of those who can be with the dying. She still feels grief when she loses her loved ones, but she does not feel fear or resentment. You can develop this ability too. Use this book, your Buddhist practice, and the insights from our twelve wise teachers, and begin training for death and grief.

The Gift of Acceptance

Seth Segall does not remember a time or a specific event when he became aware of death. His sense is that there was never really a time when he was afraid of death. For as long as he can remember, he understood death as a natural part of our life cycle.

In college, while reading about existentialism, he came across the theory that fear of death is one of our most rampant anxieties. That concept did not resonate with him. He understood that death would come and that it was a perfectly natural process. He will be the first to tell you that he knows that his innate understanding and lack of fear around death is something that sets him apart from the rest of us.

Seth's acceptance of death is a gift. It has allowed him to be with his loved ones throughout the process of their deaths. He was able to see his parents through their final moments. And after thirty-six years of marriage, when his first wife died of cancer, he was able to understand that it was her time. She had been in severe pain every day for a year. He knew that when her time came, death was a welcome release—a return to peace. His calm acceptance allowed them to have important discussions around plans for her funeral, how her eulogy would go, and what she wished to be buried in. The year of her illness was absolutely devastating for them both, but her death was a sweet release.

Diane and Seth are rare. Seth had an innate awareness of death. Diane possessed an ability to face death with equanimity at an early age. Most of us who express a significant loss so young are not ready to process it. Usually, we do not get the help we need.

Before continuing, please stop and consider that point. It is important. The ability to naturally be comfortable with death is rare. However, it is a life skill that we can develop, and as with other skills, our level of accomplishment will fluctuate. Think of it in a way that makes sense to you. Know that these are not competitive skills, they are coping skills. Our Buddhist teachings provide us lessons on how to strengthen them. As your skills strengthen, you will be able to help yourself and others.

On Processing Death

When Mary Stancavage was five years old, her father died. Her experience is very representative of a child's inability to acknowledge death and how adults cannot assist. Before her father's death, there was also a whole string of pet deaths, but she did not have enough time to make the leap from dog and cat deaths to human deaths. She was not in a place where she could acknowledge or process the emotions around losing her father. Her memory is that the whole thing was dealt with quickly and factually. It was like her mother told her, "Your father died, he is not coming home again, here's your dinner." No discussion, no allowance for questions, just keep moving.

Within seven years, Dave Smith encountered two tragic deaths. The first when he was eleven, and then again when he was eighteen. First, his sister was killed in a traffic accident on the way to school. It was shocking and devastating, and while it has been many years, his family still struggles with it today. He remembers knowing that the adults around him were in turmoil. Yet, there was this pretense that everything was okay. He was left to cope with his own suffering, in his own way. He chose drugs as his coping mechanism.

When he was beginning to see some light and had found some purpose in being a Grateful Dead hippy, his girlfriend was killed in a car accident. That was it—no more light and positivity for him. He was in a very dark place. As far as he was concerned, there was no God, no benevolent universe, just this unfair experience called life. Clearly, the deck was stacked against him. This led him to what he has described as a destructive existential philosophy of life.

In his own words, "So I had this kind of destructive existential philosophy view of, like, I'm just, you know, pardon my language, fuck everything. I'm just going to do whatever I want to do. And that's what I did. So, I became very entitled. Very self-centered, very if it's all a big nothing, then I'm just going to have fun and I'm just going to party and do drugs and play music and I'm going to do whatever I want and if people don't like it, that's their problem."

As we discussed how other people come to know about death, he pointed out,

"You know, it's not rocket science. It's not a difficult concept to grasp. You know even kids get it at some point. Everybody knows everybody dies. We all know we're going to die. The challenges come from the denial that so many people have around the obvious and natural fact of death. It is one of the most normal things that occurs in our lives, but it is also one of the most painful things. We know it, but we try not to know it. Death is real, but we are not sure how to deal with it." Like others, he sees that the tragic deaths he experienced so early in his life have helped him come to terms with impermanence—his own and that of that of his loved ones.

Aha! And there it is, in case you wondered—the reason that I am sharing these death-awareness stories with you. Yes, I want you to consider how you came to know about death. I also want you to see that not only have each of our teachers come to terms with death, but it has also moved them forward in their practice. Don't try to tell me, "But they are advanced teachers, some of them are monks or nuns." They are all human beings. Everything we will discuss in this book is accessible to you.

Monks and Nuns Learn About Death Too

Venerable Sumitta has always known death as part of his life. His father died when he was three years old. When he was nine, his seventeen-year-old sister drowned. He grew up in Sri Lanka, where Mahaweli, Kalu, Walawe, and Kelani are four major rivers. These rivers originate in the peak of the central highlands. Venerable Sumitta and his family lived in the central hill area. During certain times of the year, there would be torrential rains. During a year of heavy and severe rain, the rivers overran their banks and his sister was swept away.

His mother did not hide the deaths or avoid the deaths, but she also never let them feel like they were missing anything. She was able to balance the fact that his father was gone, and that his sister had died in a beautiful way. His mother worked hard to be everything—breadwinner, supporter, and nurturer. If there was a gap left behind by these deaths, she found ways to fill it.

When he was eleven, Venerable Sumitta became a monk. His responsibilities included attending funerals. Even when he was not officiating, he was still attending, and seeing people in their grief. He found that when he saw people from his community cry, he too, would cry. Because he was so young, he began to fear funerals. Seeing people in the depth of their sorrows was frightening. One day he said to his teacher, "I don't want to go to funerals. I'm scared of them." His teacher denied his request and continued to require him to attend the funerals in the community. Hearing so many people crying so loudly was very disturbing for the young monk. As he grew older, he would understand that this intense crying was a healing release for the friends and family of the deceased. He learned that he was witnessing a natural process. He also realized that learning about death was an important part of his training.

In 1999, when his father died, Venerable De Hong had one of his first strong and personal encounters with death. He would not become a Buddhist monk for another seven years. His father had been physically and emotionally abusive, and what

Venerable De faced was a reconciliation of the trauma that he carried due to this abuse. His experience was one of self-healing and of recognition that he was now free from that abusive relationship. Eventually, he would feel forgiveness toward his father, but first he had to allow himself to acknowledge his own trauma.

In 2006, when he became a monk, Venerable De began to have new experiences with death. He spent eighteen months in Vietnam, and he recalls that there was a funeral every day. This really solidified his acceptance of death as part of our life cycle. When he returned to Southern California, he was called on to attend or help officiate funeral services on a regular basis. Death was part of his life, and part of his practice as a monk.

Despite his daily interactions with death, his mother's cancer diagnosis in 2014 was still difficult to process. He remembers thinking, "Wow, this is real. The woman who gave birth to me could die." His openness in discussing how he felt when his father died and how death was still a bit of an abstract even though he attended daily funerals is so refreshing. We think we know death; we think we are comfortable with it, and yet, our relationship with death is complex. It is a multilayered, multifaceted relationship. Do not be surprised if your reactions to death vary. Being aware of death and forming a friendship with death does not mean that you will be unaffected by it, and it does not mean that your emotions will be consistent. It means that you will be open to the depth and breadth of what comes your way. You will be able to just be with your experience, seeking to let go of judgment and opening up to insight.

If you really want to meet death, try being bitten by a poisonous snake. In 1989, while walking in the forest of the Himalayas, Venerable Karma Lekshe Tsomo was bitten by a poisonous viper. Her right arm became swollen with gangrene. She spent months in a hospital in Delhi, enduring treatments and surgeries, and alternatively contemplating her own death or life with the use of just one arm. Ultimately, she prevailed and gained use of her arm. She also gained considerable insight into the nature of impermanence.

Long before the snakebite, came the loss of her beloved dog, Scampi. She describes him as a smart and loving dog. But he was no match for the Pacific Coast Highway at night. She was devastated by the loss of her furry best friend. And she was confused. Where did he go? Why did he have to go? What kind of world is this where a sweet and loving dog encounters such an unfair death? Raised in a Christian family, she turned to the ministers at her church for answers. What she learned was that if you are good, you go to heaven, and if you are bad, you go to hell.

Her elders were trying to streamline the information, to make it more understandable for a young girl whose dog had died. It was too simplistic. What her elders did not realize was that she was ready to receive deeper teachings and insights. Interestingly, her dissatisfaction with the teachings she received about death would become one of the reasons she would later become drawn to Buddhism. Her first day in a class at the Institute of the Library of Tibetan Works in Dharamshala she found herself learning all about the detailed stages of the dying process. She stayed and studied there for six years.

While she lay recovering from that snakebite, everything she had learned helped her accept her possible death, and to fully understand the practices on death and impermanence. She truly transcended theory and went into the experiential. Please know, snakebites are not necessarily a recommended part of the path!

It would be unusual if you have not had your own introduction to death. Think back to the time when you first became aware of death—what was it like? Do any of the experiences of our teachers resonate with you? It is critical that you do not ignore your encounters with death. These encounters are lessons. Remember, we are building some important coping skills. Timber expressed this in such a helpful way:

"Life itself prepares us gradually in the sense that as children, first, you know, like your goldfish dies and then maybe your dog dies and then maybe your grandparents and then maybe your parents or friends or whatnot, everyone's got a different order. But It starts out very gradual and as I said in the beginning, if we don't learn to deal with it in a healthy fashion at a young age, and we sweep it under the rug. We don't talk about it. We don't address it. We don't unpack it then later in life when it's something bigger than a goldfish or a pet or someone who is a distant relative then it hits us really hard because it's the first time, we're talking about it, facing it, addressing it. I'm in a way glad I was raised in a country where death was a part of everyday life. When people say we'll cross that bridge when we get there. I think they're overlooking the fact that we are all on that bridge."

We are here together, on the bridge. Don't jump. Keep walking. Or in this case, keep reading. In the chapters to come, you will be able to share the experiences of death with some wise and wonderful people. This book is your opportunity to strengthen yourself, and to continue to build your skills. You can be death ready and support yourself and others. How? It all starts with you and your practice. You are in training.

Chapter 3

Training for Death

Both Mary Stancavage and Diane Wilde teach a course called *A Year to Live*. When I first spoke to Mary, she told me that death was one of her favorite topics. This is because of the help she received as a participant in the *A Year to Live* course several years ago. She found it to be transformational. The course takes the perspective that you have received a terminal diagnosis, and this is the last year of your life. It really is about coming to grips with dying. Taking that deep look at your life and considering, "If I die today, is this what I want my life to be?" Mary has now facilitated quite a few groups through this practice. She appreciates that it really is an in-depth investigation of "I am of the nature to die," from the Five Recollections.

Diane has seen the difficulty that comes from failure to accept the possibility of our own deaths. An especially difficult death for her to observe was that of a close family member. He was very close to the end and still unwilling to consider his own death. He would not talk about his feelings or allow anyone else to broach the subject. He kept insisting that he could live for another twenty years. As she told me this story, I expressed that I really hoped that he went peacefully in his sleep. But he did not—he was agitated and fighting until the very end. He did not have a peaceful death.

Both Mary and Diane emphasized that *A Year to Live* not only helps you become comfortable with death, but the course also helps you enjoy your life to the fullest. Many of those who take the course are not terminally ill—they are simply curious and open to the experience.

When we learned that he was terminal, my husband Ed and I signed up to take this course with a teacher here in Southern California. In the capriciousness of death, Ed did not live long enough to start the course. Perhaps I will take it another time.

The Five Recollections

Seth Segall and his first wife had their own very personal experience of *A Year to Live*. Together they went through her diagnosis, illness, and eventual death from cancer. He told me that in some ways during that time, they had never been closer. They were together almost all the time. He accompanied her to the doctor's office and helped with her care. They both knew what was coming. Some days were full of tears, some were full of laughter, and some had both. He began to look at it like the weather. Some days it is sunny, some days it is stormy, but it is all part of the journey. What he learned was to accept each day as it came and to take it as it was, with no expectations around how things were supposed to be. Like Mary and Diane, Seth also found the Five Recollections to be helpful. When we were talking, he read me a version by Thich Nhat Hanh:

> *I am of the nature to grow old.*
> *There is no way to escape growing old.*
> *I am of the nature to have ill health.*
> *There is no way to escape that will help.*
> *I am of the nature to die.*
> *There is no way to escape to death.*

> *All that is dear to me and everyone I love are of the nature of change.*
> *There was no way to escape being separated from them.*
> *My actions are my only true belongings.*
> *I cannot escape the consequences of my actions.*
> *My actions are the ground upon which I stand.*
> (From the *Plum Village Chanting*, by Thich Nhat Hanh)

To sum it up in a more humorous way, Seth recalled a cartoon he saw several years ago. The image was of a movie theater marquee, and the coming attraction it announced was, "Coming soon to a neighborhood near you, old age, sickness, and death."

For Cayce Howe, living at a meditation center was a beautiful training ground for looking at death. It happened that his cabin was right next door to the hospice cabin. It is funny that I never knew this until we sat down together to capture his thoughts for this book. Cayce is a teacher at a local group where I meditate, and he came to the house and meditated with Ed and me during Ed's hospice.

Cayce lived next door to the dying for two years. Most days, there was someone staying in that cabin, and often Cayce would be the first one to realize that his neighbor had died. He had a constant reminder of impermanence and plenty of opportunity to meditate on death. During this time, Cayce learned a teaching from Lama Zopa Rinpoche that he would eventually pass on to Ed and me. "Don't forget that living people are dying before dying people every day." Somebody in hospice care might make it to the end of the day, while someone who is deemed healthy may not. We do not know when there will be an accident or an unforeseen health issue. This is meant to inspire us to keep practicing. You are fortunate to have the causes and conditions today for practice, and nothing is guaranteed.

On Helping Others

There are ways in which you can help someone through his or her final days. You can help by listening to stories. You can help by asking about his or her life. You can acknowledge his or her accomplishments—some that occur to you while listening and learning, and some that he or she specifically mentions. You can assist with phone calls or arrange virtual discussions with others. You can help with letter writing. You can read favorite books or poems. Play comforting music. Just be there; just listen. It does not have to be more complicated than that. And be grateful to be a part of their final days. Venerable Karma Lekshe Tsomo showed me another reason to appreciate the dying:

"Whenever we experience a loss, a death of a friend or a loved one or even an acquaintance. We can consider that to be very fortunate in the sense that it wakes us up, it wakes us up to the reality of life, and that's the real beauty of doing meditation on death. It reminds us of the preciousness of every moment of life. Human life is something very special, difficult to attain and very tenuous, we can use it, especially now, we all know every day we're alive. It's a blessing. And so, when someone passes away, we can thank them because they've helped us to remember the importance of being aware and being thankful for every precious moment."

Bring your gratitude into the room; bring your happy memories. Do not bring your disappointment, or false expectations for him or her to rally. Death is not a failure. And you do not want to pressure the dying with your fears and pending grief. What you can do is help him or her focus on their breath, and to breathe together, calmly and carefully, in and out, in and out. This helps bring peace to all of you, but most importantly, to the one who is dying. A peaceful death will help lead to a better rebirth.

Not everyone is going to have a peaceful death. Seth Segall's first mother-in-law had a near-death experience two weeks before she died. While some experience a feeling of peace and seeing a loving light, she felt suffocated by the smell of roses and fought to get back into her body. She wanted to stay if possible. She was willing to try every treatment and surgery that was available to prolong her life. Timber Hawkeye shared an expression about the clinging and attachment that so many of us experience: "Everything that I have ever let go of had claw marks on it." Our practice, our training for death, is about learning to let go, and to help others do the same.

If your loved one did not have a peaceful death, do not despair over how he or she died. That is behind you. Engage in good works with pure intention and you can generate merit that you can transfer. And that merit may reach the deceased and may help offset the fact that he or she did not have a peaceful death. Your merit also helps you achieve a better rebirth.

> *With mind rightly directed,*
> *speaking right speech,*
> *doing right deeds with the body:*
> *a person here of much learning,*
> *a doer of merit*
> *here in this life so short,*
> *at the break-up of the body,*
> *discerning, reappears in heaven. (Iti 71)*

By invoking right speech and taking skillful actions and developing right concentration, you can become a doer of merit. Seeking to generate merit is not selfish. It is a skillful way to advance in your practice—the correct application of generosity, virtue, and meditation combined with giving can lead to happiness and can also minimize the negative impact of past karma. There is a passage in the Itivuttaka that reminds us that when we store away wealth and material things to safeguard against future losses, we risk losing those resources. But when we create a storehouse of merit there can be no loss.

> *But when a man or woman*
> *has laid aside a well-stored fund*
> *of generosity, virtue,*
> *restraint, and self-control,*
> *with regard to a shrine,*
> *the Sangha,*
> *a fine individual,*
> *guests,*
> *mother, father,*
> *or elder sibling:*
> *That's a well-stored fund.*
> *It can't be wrested away.*
> *It follows you along.*
> *When, having left this world,*
> *for wherever you must go,*
> *you take it with you.*
> *This fund is not held in common with others,*
> *and cannot be stolen by thieves.*
> *So, enlightened, you should make merit,*
> *the fund that will follow you along.*
> *This is the fund*
> *that gives all they want*
> *to beings human, divine. (Khp 8)*

When you advance in your practice, you can be of more benefit to others. It is critical that you do good acts for the right reasons, and that you give to the right recipients. Some will give gifts and receive little or no merit. Others will enjoy the fruits of their giving. It all comes back to your intention. If you can give without seeking profit for yourself, looking for a reward, or actively trying to build a storehouse of merit, you are more likely to receive merit. There are some passages in the Aṅguttara Nikāya that provide helpful insight about skillful giving.

Consider reading AN 7:49, AN 5:148, and AN 5:36. Another useful resource is "Merit: The Buddha's Strategies for Happiness," a study guide prepared by Thanissaro Bhikkhu.

You can seek to dedicate the merit you accrue to those who have died before you. And in the right situation, they might receive your merit. This is an area where I have heard different teachings. I recommend that you speak with your teacher, and research the dedication of merit as it applies to your specific practice. As I have come to understand it, there is no guarantee that I can send merit directly to a specific person—unless that person is in one of the possible places. The teaching on possible versus impossible places is rather long, and might not be relevant to your practice. You can find a passage on the impossible places in Aṅguttara Nikāya 10:177.

If you are the one who is dying. You can help your loved ones. You can acknowledge that your final day is approaching, and you can share your thoughts and feelings with your friends and family. You do not have to do this alone. To the extent that you have the capacity, you can help with your own arrangements. Try to let those who are closest to you understand your preferences. My parents did such a good job with all the business and materialistic aspects of their deaths. Everything was well organized. What a relief. I never knew that I would be taking care of my mother's death while also coping with my husband's death. In both instances, I had a full understanding of what each of them wanted. You can ease the burden for your people if your wishes are known and your paperwork is up to date and easy to find. It will be enough for the ones you leave behind to work with their grief.

Do You Have a Training Plan?

Each of our wise teachers advocates training yourself to deal with death. You may think, "I'll deal with that when the time comes." That is your right. This is like choosing to run a marathon with no training. Even though you rarely even jog around the block, you go out there and attempt to run all 26 miles and 385 yards. You might make it to the finish line, but it is going to hurt.

As you move through life, you will have more and more experiences with death. You can choose to accept this as part of your life, or you can spend more time in denial. Do not waste your energy.

> *Make the day not-in-vain,*
> *a little or a lot.*
> *However much*
> *the day passes,*
> *that's how much less*
> *is life.*
> *Your last day approaches.*
> *This isn't your time*
> *to be heedless. (Thag 6.13)*

The clock is ticking. The date for that marathon approaches. An athlete follows a training program designed to build his or her strength and endurance. Each part of that program is geared toward setting them up to participate in a specific event successfully.

Suppose you faced the death of a close family member at an early age. Consider revisiting your training and consider becoming a coach to others.

Perhaps, as a child, you dealt with the loss of your favorite pet. Then, later, a grandparent. Or one of your friends had a death in the family. You have begun your training and now it is time for you to get back to work. Here is a high-level plan for your consideration.

Training Level One:

Impermanence

If you follow the lesson on impermanence to its natural conclusion, it is not just your thoughts and emotions that are rising and falling. Everything is rising and falling. Every one of us rises and ultimately falls. It is important to remember that *everyone* is going to experience death.

Recognize that everything will change. We are *all* subject to old age, sickness, and death. Old age is a gift. The more you can become comfortable with the knowledge that you cannot keep everything and everyone you love, and that you cannot avoid the things you do not enjoy, the closer you are to the end of suffering.

It is not just good times and bad times that will pass; we will too. It is useful to work with the phrases, *we too shall pass, I too shall pass, Mom and Dad too shall pass*, and *[beloved friend/partner] too shall pass*. It is not about *whether* you and your loved ones will die. It is about *when* you and your loved ones will die.

Training Level Two:

Keep Death in Mind

You would do well to spend time considering death and thinking that today could be your last day. That this could be the last day of someone you love. The purpose of this practice is not to dwell in a place of morbidity but to appreciate the preciousness of the life you have been given. To be born as a human being is a gift. In this lifetime, you can practice the dharma. After you die, you might lose this opportunity.

You can save yourself a tremendous amount of pain with some preparation. You do not have to walk around obsessed with death; just hold the possibility of death in your thoughts.

Think about death throughout your day. Use death as a meditation device. Consider the phrase, *today could be my last day*. Death is just one of many experiences that make up a life. It is neither good nor bad. It just is.

One way you can make it easier is to accept death as an integral part of life. A way to accept death into your life is to allow yourself to think about it. Don't turn off thoughts about losing others. Don't turn away from people who have experienced loss. Be part of that experience. Ignoring people who are sick does not make them well. Refusing to acknowledge death does not make you or anyone else immortal. The more you wish to avoid suffering, the harder it will be. And the more you crave or want for the people you love never to have to leave you, the more difficult it will be when they do.

Training Level Three:

Practice the Five Recollections

The Five Recollections combine a healthy recognition of impermanence with death awareness. Like a good training plan, Level Three is drawing from the foundation you built for yourself in levels one and two. Most of the Buddhist monks and nuns that I know chant these recollections every day. Place these recollections where you will see them and remember to recite them. Please pay attention to these words and the impact they have on you. Use them in your meditation practice.

Training Level Four:

Meditate on Death

Meditating on your death and the death of your loved ones is beneficial. It is also challenging. That is why this is level four of your training plan. When my father told me that his lung cancer was terminal, I meditated on his death. Not so much on the actual moment of his death, but on the fact that he would die. I meditated on him being dead and how I would feel about it. I shed many tears, but it helped me to wrap my head around the fact that he was dying. I used the same approach when my husband was dying.

Long before you have a loved one with a terminal diagnosis, you can develop a solid *maraṇasati* or mindfulness of death practice. In the *Satipatthana Sutta (MN 10)*, instructions are given on how to contemplate the body as a body that has been disposed of in the charnel ground. Remember that just as that body has met various stages of decay, so too will your body. Your body is no different from that body in the charnel ground.

The *Kāyagatāsati Sutta (MN 119)* teaches mindfulness of the body and again refers to charnel ground contemplation to remind us of the impermanence and dissolution we all face.

The *Maraṇasati Sutta (AN 6.20)* emphasizes the importance of the mindfulness of death. Not just because it makes it easier for us to deal with death, but also because it reminds us to be more dedicated to our spiritual practice.

These are not hidden teachings, they are commonly taught in many parts of the world, yet they could be new to you. And if that is the case, remember to seek out a qualified teacher and practice with your local Buddhist community.

Take this training plan and give it a try. Make adjustments that will make it more useful for you. Note that I did not say make adjustments that will make it easier for you. You do not run a successful marathon based on a series of easy sprints. Know that each time you encounter death, your experience will be a bit different. And if you approach each death from a place of openness, you will improve your practice. You will become stronger. Please remember to keep up with your training. You are not finished until your last race is run.

Chapter 4

Death Has Many Faces

Most of my experiences with death have been with family members who had terminal illnesses. Once they were diagnosed, I knew death was coming. I did not know the exact time of day that their death would occur, but I could see that it was coming. And even though my mother died of a sudden heart attack, it was in some ways not a surprise. She was eighty-six, and she had lived for two years without my father. There was a degree of understanding that it was her time.

Sometimes death comes suddenly. Death comes to the young and healthy. Death can seem capricious. This is a reminder of the value of our practice. There is no way to prepare ourselves for all the different ways death may arrive in our lives, and we shouldn't try. Instead, we should rely on the Four Noble Truths, become comfortable with impermanence, and use the pertinent teachings from your school of Buddhism.

You may be in a different state for each death that you encounter. Some will knock you off balance in ways you did not expect. Some may lead you to question the fairness of it all. Each of them will teach you, if you are open to the lesson.

Euthanasia and Suicide

Long before he became ill, my husband used to say that if he ever found out that he was terminally ill, he would move someplace where euthanasia was allowed, and take charge of his death. This was very upsetting to me. When he was diagnosed as terminal, I broached the subject. I was extremely nervous. If I could not keep him alive, I would help him have the death that he wanted to have. To my relief, he had changed his mind. He said that he knew there was not going to be any miracle that would save him, but he was going to live his life to its natural ending. He was going to see his karma through.

Diane Wilde's elderly father went through two major operations. He was tired, and he was ready to die. He read the book, *Final Exit: The Practicalities of Self-Deliverance and Assisted Suicide for the Dying*. He asked Diane if she would help him with his euthanasia. She agreed but prayed that he would not really ask her to go through with it. Fortunately for both of them, shortly after he asked for her help, he died of a heart attack in his sleep. He died with a big smile on his face. Her mother told her that she did not realize he was dead because he looked so happy.

Some people have taken charge of their own deaths. Timber Hawkeye recalls attending death parties during the AIDS pandemic. This was a time when being diagnosed with AIDS was a definitive death sentence. For most, it was a painful and horrible death. Some would be surrounded by friends, but many were abandoned by friends or family. Rather than have this experience, some chose a death on their own terms. They would have one big last party. It was a goodbye party, although often nobody acknowledged it. When the party was over, they would kill themselves.

Timber shared with me that to cope with all of that death, he would pretend that his friend had moved to Europe. And in this way, he was able to confront the fact that he was not going to see his friend again. In his mind Europe was very far away. Later, Timber was able to recognize that what his friend had done was to choose going into the unknown of death now, instead of a known death of suffering later. There is something appealing about spending your final moments having a good time with your loved ones and letting them know that you love and appreciate them.

Now Timber accepts that the reality is much greater than Europe, his friends went into the great unknown. They went on the ultimate adventure that we all get to go on.

There is not one Buddhist position on euthanasia. There is not one Buddhism. There are different schools and many teachers, and therefore many opinions. A concern that might be considered prevalent is that if you take your death into your own hands, you are not allowing your karma to ripen naturally, and this may lead you to a difficult rebirth, one with similar suffering. If you or your loved one is considering euthanasia, conduct your research carefully. Try to sit with your thoughts and emotions for as long as possible. If you are opposed to euthanasia, express your concerns, and try not to place your judgments on others. You do not need to participate if your participation violates your beliefs. You also do not want to add to someone else's burden, or act in a way that makes death less peaceful.

In reflecting on the suicide of her favorite aunt, Holly Hisamoto says, "You know, so with suicide death. It's often . . . second-guessing things and thinking it's my fault or what could I do differently or a lot of that stuff. Feelings of guilt, feelings of anger. You know, so with suicide death. Feeling abandoned." She also expressed that suicide is not commonly discussed. Sometimes families do not want to reveal how their loved one died. It is a type of disenfranchisement. It is complex and multilayered, and these layers become part of the family story. Her experience is that there is a heaviness that still lives within her family.

As with euthanasia, there is not one overarching Buddhist position on suicide. There are similar concerns around not allowing your karma to ripen naturally. Clearly there are spiritual consequences. There is a rule for monks, prohibiting them from purposefully depriving another human of life, from praising the advantages of death, or inciting others to take their own lives. This can be extended to laypeople as well. In the United States there are legal ramifications for pushing someone toward suicide. As Holly pointed out, when your loved one chooses suicide, you will be left with many difficult emotions. Perhaps one day you will be able to let go of everything but love for the person who took his or her own life.

Losing Our Parents

As my classmate, friend, and colleague at the nonprofit Engaged Buddhist Alliance, Venerable De saw me through the death of both my parents and my husband. At the time that we met, his father was long gone. Soon enough, he would lose his mother. When your parents are gone, it is a strange feeling. Venerable De remembers that when learning of his mother's terminal cancer diagnosis, he thought, "Who will love me unconditionally now?" And I recall thinking after both my parents were dead, "Wow, now I really am an orphan." In some ways it was an odd thought. I am a grown woman. If I had children, they would also be adults. But it was like temporarily returning to the state of being five years old. Most of us are going to experience the loss of our parents. The other alternative is much more difficult, that one or both of our parents experience the death of their child.

Venerable De's advice is to face it. Be aware of your feelings and your sense of loss, and let it rise. Face it head-on. Feel whatever you need to feel and say whatever you need to say, and know that it will not be easy. As a Buddhist monk, he was taught about death, and trained for the acceptance of death, but he is both a monk and a human being.

In a similar discussion with Venerable Sumitta, he reminded me that the Buddha missed his own mother after she died. He visited her in the Tusita heaven and preached the dharma to her. The Buddha emphasized the importance of honoring and caring for your parents.

> *Mother and father,*
> *compassionate to their family,*
> *are called*
> > *Brahma,*
> > *first teachers,*
> > *those worthy of gifts*
> > *from their children.*
> *So the wise should pay them*
> > > *homage,*
> > > *honor*
> > *with food and drink*
> > *clothing and bedding*
> > *anointing and bathing*
> > *and washing their feet.*
> *Performing these services to their parents,*
> *the wise*
> *are praised right here*
> *and after death*
> *rejoice in heaven. (Iti 4.7)*

Taking care of your parents is like caring for the Buddha himself. Today, countries that are traditionally Buddhist have a longstanding practice of caring for their parents. Growing up in

Sri Lanka, Venerable Sumitta was taught a daily practice of saluting his mother. (His father died when he was a toddler.) Every night before he would go to sleep, he would bow to his mother and recite a stanza from the Pāli Canon.

He remembers that one day he went to bed without paying his respects to his mother. In the middle of the night, he woke up, and he realized his mistake. He went to her bed and paid his respects. Of course, this woke her up, but she was not angry. She just touched his head, and when he finished, she sent him back to bed.

Death and Privilege

"Death is a pleasure to common and middlemen. Only rich and powerful men worry much about death. They are always in glass houses for protection." (Anonymous)

A listener of *The Death Dhamma Podcast* left the above comment for me. With appreciation that someone took the time to share his or her thoughts with me, I read it a few times to process it. Here are three of my takeaways:

This person was telling me that spending time discussing death was a pursuit for the privileged.

If you are not privileged, death might be welcome.

Only wealthy people worry about death, and they try to protect themselves from death, but their attempts are futile (glass houses).

There is an amount of social inequity in death. There are entire groups of people whose expectation around longevity are different than mine, whose experiences with end-of-life care are different than mine. As my listener pointed out, to the less fortunate, death might be a pleasure. Peace after a difficult life. Maybe not the path to their deaths, but the concept of death represents the end of a life full of struggle.

The concept of inequity in death surfaced in my discussions with Holly Hisamoto, Venerable Karma Lekshe Tsomo, and Diane Wilde.

The way in which Holly broached it was that as a hospice worker, she was in a relationship with planned death. With people who had access to a good level of care, and the ability to receive physical, emotional, and spiritual care to help them have a peaceful death. My family members also were in a relationship with planned death. And while there was a difference between the competencies of the hospice teams we worked with, there was never a doubt that we would have help. We had access to excellent medical care, at-home hospice care, counseling services, and spiritual care. I understand that it is due to privilege that these services were available to us, and still it was difficult. Imagine how much more difficult it is for those who do not have the same privilege?

There are people whose lives end due to racial violence, or because of poverty and lack of access to health care. What some of us might consider to be an untimely death, is an everyday occurrence in their world. There is a social justice element to death. Death is not just about my family members and lung cancer, or my elderly mother's heart attack. We see unjust deaths occurring every day. Far too often they are the result of social injustice, and it is not enough to see this as someone's karma coming to fruition.

My discussion with Holly reminded me of a story. This story comes from an amazing spiritual teacher, a man who really puts his beliefs into practice in a positive and tangible way. I am talking about Father Gregory Boyle, S. J., founder of Homeboy Industries, the world's largest gang intervention and rehabilitation program.

In his book, *Tattoos on the Heart: The Power of Boundless Compassion*, he tells the story of being at a party with some of the young men and women from Homeboys. One of the young ladies has a on a very pretty party dress. Father Boyle tells her that she looks great. She looks at him, thanks him, and informs him that this is the dress she wants to be buried in. Initially, this strikes him as odd because it may look a little weird when she is eighty-five to be buried in this dress. Later, he comes to an important realization. She has no expectation of being buried as an old lady. She expects to die at an age when that dress is still appropriate.

Do not look on those who are less fortunate from a place of superiority, thinking, "This is their experience because they have bad karma; they earned it." Karma stems from your actions in your past lives, past actions from this life, and your current actions. When you experience negative karma, all you can do is work on your current actions. You cannot go back in time and undo the actions that contributed to your negative karma. There is no place for blame in karma. Karma is not an excuse for lack of action. Suppose you look away because there have always been poverty and social injustice. Then you do not truly understand karma. Skillful actions that will help you create your own karma involve helping others. Engage in skillful actions now. Skillful actions do not involve turning your back on others.

When you act to help end systemic racism, and social and financial inequity, you are helping others have peaceful deaths. If after sitting with death, and working on your own training, you still find it difficult to be with the dying, you can work in areas that will be of benefit. If you help create a world where others can have a better life path, you are also helping them with death. If you volunteer in a program that makes education more accessible to at-risk youth, more of those young people will continue their educations, and earn degrees or participate in vocational training. They are more likely to be able to support themselves in ways that allow them to exit a cycle of violence and incarceration. They will have better access to some of the services that people like me take for granted. A peaceful life is more likely to lead to a peaceful death.

If you live a life where you have the time to practice, and to prepare for death, you are privileged. There is quite a bit that needed to fall into place for you to be able to practice. You had to be born as a human being, in a time and place where you had access to Buddhist teachings, and you had to be able to heed those teachings. This passage points out the rarity of it all:

> *Monks, suppose that this great earth were totally covered with water, and a man were to toss a yoke with a single hole there. A wind from the east would push it west, a wind from the west would push it east. A wind from the north would push it south, a wind from the south would push it north. And suppose a blind sea-turtle were there. It would come to the surface once every one hundred years. Now what do you think: would that blind sea-turtle, coming to the surface once every one hundred years, stick his neck into the yoke with a single hole?*
>
> *It would be a sheer coincidence, lord, that the blind sea-turtle, coming to the surface once every one hundred years, would stick his neck into the yoke with a single hole.*
>
> *It's likewise a sheer coincidence that one obtains the human state. It's likewise a sheer coincidence that a Tathagata, worthy and rightly self-awakened, arises in the world. It's likewise a sheer coincidence that a doctrine and discipline expounded by a Tathagata appears in the world. Now, this human state has been obtained. A Tathagata, worthy and rightly self-awakened, has arisen in the world. A doctrine and*

> *discipline expounded by a Tathagata appears in the world.*
>
> *Therefore your duty is the contemplation, "This is stress . . . This is the origination of stress . . . This is the cessation of stress." Your duty is the contemplation, "This is the path of practice leading to the cessation of stress." (SN 56.48)*

Dying Alone

An image circulated on social media that cut right to the heart of death during the COVID-19 pandemic. Two members of a medical team stand at a hospital window. Both are fully garbed in protective gear—they wear what looks like hazmat suits, their heads are concealed within hoods, and masks cover their mouths and noses. You can just barely make out their eyes. Each of them holds a sign up to the window. One reads: "He is at peace now." The other: "We are so sorry." We are left to wonder just how many friends and family members are outside reading the signs. We know that because of the concerns around spreading COVID-19, they could not have held their loved one's hand as he died.

Due to social distancing restrictions, there are many stories of family members hospitalized and dying without their loved ones seeing or speaking to them again. Or family members saying goodbye using FaceTime or hearing final breaths over the phone. And for many of us, our grief is intensified because we think that the people we love could die alone. Many of us are afraid that we, too, will die alone.

Dying alone is not a new phenomenon. Some of us will die at home in our sleep, or in a hospital bed when nobody is in the room, or in some other way without others present. Why do we have such an aversion to solitary death? Perhaps we are afraid of the unknown, and we want to have others to help us face it. We project this fear on to others, so we do not want them to be alone, and, most dangerously, we assume that we will be given that final moment to say, "I love you," or "I forgive you," or "Thank you," or "Please forgive me." However, when it comes to death, it is best not to make assumptions. This is what we know:

> *Those who have come to be,*
> *those who will be,*
> *All will go,*
> *leaving the body behind.*
> *The skillful person,*
> *realizing the loss of all,*
> should live the holy life ardently. (Ud 5.2)

Men and women in prison lose family members all the time. They cannot be there—not for the death, and not for the funeral. Diane Wilde, who has taught Buddhism in prison for over seventeen years encourages them to talk to their dead, and to tell them exactly how they feel. She tells them that it is possible that their deceased loved ones can hear them. She has them create and recite mantras to honor them. She has seen this practice benefit her students time and time again. Diane is teaching them reconciliation.

> *Some do not understand that we must die,*
> *But those who do realize this*
> *Settle their quarrels. (Dhp 6)*

Reconcile where you can, and where you cannot reconcile, make peace with it yourself. Much of this is about your need for a last-minute apology or goodbye or to tell someone that you love them. If they always know that you love them, you eliminate this regret.

If your loved one dies and you cannot be with him or her, and you cannot have an official service, then create one of your own. Work with others to create a remembrance or celebration that captures their spirit and helps you with your grief. You might hold an online vigil and share his or her favorite images and music. You might form a temporary book club and read his or her favorite book. Or commit to meditating each day at a specific time in his or her honor. We live in rapidly changing times, seek to find solutions that bring you more peace and build kinship. And as you regain your strength, consider how you can help others who will have the same experience.

The only guarantee is that we *will* die. Dying alone is not the same thing as dying lonely. Learn how to be peaceful at the time of your death. Practice diligently. When you come to peace around death, you will know that it does not matter who is or is not next to you when you take your last breath.

Try to Bring Peace

Some of us can be in a hospice facility and still be in denial. Or our friends and family members can be in denial. Even in hospice, death can come suddenly. There is an expression that Cayce Howe used to say to Ed and me while meditating with us during Ed's hospice, "The living are dying, and the dying are living." Some people, like the young lady in the party dress, know this, it is within the core of their being. It would be nice to live in a world where that is not her reality, but I admire her ability to see her world as it is.

We can help set the tone for someone as they die. One way to do this is to not burden the dying with our sadness or disappointment. Death is an inevitability; it is not a failure. Venerable Karma Lekshe Tsomo, expressed it like this, "In our youth culture, we've come to expect everyone to be, you know, to be young forever, which is totally unrealistic." This makes us closed off to aging, illness, and death. No matter how we experience death, it is due to our karma. I am not the right one to give a full exposition on karma and exactly how it works. I do offer up this reminder, your karma is a blend of your past and current actions. In past lives and in this one. You cannot undo the past, what you can do is be the best person that you can be today.

When you see a child who dies from cancer, saying that this was his or her karma can seem as hollow as saying, "Well, everything happens for a reason." Yes, everything happens for a reason, and that reason is karma. But please, let's not turn karma into blame. Do not blame an eight-year-old for his or her death.

Timber Hawkeye tells of a discussion where someone said that he believed that the hardest thing for a parent to have to go through is the death of a child. No parent wants their child to die before they do. Someone else in the group disagreed and said that the hardest thing for a parent to go through is to have a child who is still alive but wants nothing to do with you. This really resonated with Timber. His opinion is that nobody does death to you. The person who died did not purposefully do something to hurt you. But if someone is still alive, choosing not to be part of your life, opting to disconnect from you, that causes a very specific kind of grief. A non-death that feels very much like a death. In this case, it is possible that your person will return to you. Or not. *Metta* practice can help you come to terms with estranged friends and family members. This is a meditation practice that involves the recitation of good wishes toward yourself and toward others. *Metta*, or good will, is the antidote to ill will.

You are going to face death. And like our wise teachers, you will see many kinds of death. There will be terminal illness, and there may be euthanasia and suicide. Some deaths will seem very sudden. Some people will be very old, and others very, very young. Sometimes death will be exactly as you thought it would be—your grandfather with heart disease dies from heart disease. Other times it will be an unexpected virus or an accident. Let go of expected scenarios. These are, in their own way, a form of clinging. All you really need to know is that there will be death. And in that awareness, there is peace.

Chapter 5

Grief Has Many Faces Too

Venerable De found that for him, grief can be different each time. For example, when his father died, it brought him face-to-face with decades of trauma. In life, his father had been a harsh and abusive man. Now he knows that his father had his own kind of suffering, and this led him to be physically and emotionally abusive to his children. As the oldest child, Venerable De bore the brunt of this abuse.

As Venerable De experienced the death of his father, it was as if all this trauma came rushing up to greet him. He felt it in his head and in his body, and it took years of work to flush it out of his system.

When his mother died, he felt more peace. He was able to face her death in a calm manner. He still experienced very powerful emotions. A raw sadness. And a feeling of loss. He recalls thinking that this person who has loved me unconditionally is gone, and I am alone. Sometimes he felt empty, and not in the Buddhist experience of emptiness. Rather in the feeling of knowing that something meaningful had been lost.

A couple of weeks after his mother died, Venerable De attended a group meeting at University of the West. The purpose of the meeting was to grow in leadership, and to be able to have difficult conversations in a loving and peaceful way. He sat with a group of twelve others. When the discussion turned toward describing suffering, he mentioned his mother's death. Suddenly he was overtaken by tears. He recalls that he could not have held those tears in if he wanted to. And now, he realizes that this was the best possible time and place to express the grief that he had been feeling. Sometimes that is how grief is for many of us. We are going about our business, and then *boom*, sadness comes. And you cry. Let those tears come out. You do not need to hide them or suppress them, and you do not need to apologize for being a human being who is grieving.

I wish I had Venerable De's strength and sense. I remember walking around after the death of my family and just thinking, "Don't ask me. Don't ask me." Because if anybody said anything, I knew I would cry, and I did not want to cry. The result was that after suppressing crying for so long, when I needed to cry, I couldn't cry. I was broken. I would start crying, and then I would just stop. I would think to myself, "You need to cry, and this is a good time to do it, so come on, cry." Well, it turns out, you cannot always schedule crying time. Now I can laugh at myself for this. And if you too have tried to schedule your sad time, it is OK. Do not be hard on yourself. We all approach this in our own way, and we learn what supports our grieving process.

Grief is a very personal process. Each of the monks and nuns who shared their wisdom for this book expressed that grief is difficult for *all* of us. It can be traumatizing for anyone, no matter what training or background you have. While much of our focus together is on death, we grieve many things. Relationships, jobs, material objects, and past experiences. Don't think that grief will not impact your mental health, because it absolutely will. Be aware of changes in your thoughts and your behaviors. It is not reasonable for you to think that your daily life will be the same. Be honest about behaviors that are helpful versus harmful. If you are unclear, speak with a trusted teacher, friend, or therapist.

Your Buddhist practice can help you prepare for the idea of death, and it can help you while you are grieving. Know that most of us are still going to experience grief. Do not judge yourself harshly because you experience sadness and loss. Remember, only a stone has no feelings.

During our discussion, Venerable Guan Zhen and I learned that we both lost our fathers in 2012. We had been students together at University of the West, but in 2012, he had already moved on. He recalls how for the first few days his body took over. He felt sadness from his head to his toes, in his muscles and in his bones. The first night, he could not stop crying. The monks he lived with in the monastery kindly allowed him to have some quiet time to himself to fully feel his grief. He describes the physical pain as feeling like he had been shot in the heart with an arrow.

Buddhism Is Not a Silver Bullet

Buddhism does not necessarily stop the pain of grief. It helps us understand it, sit with it, and fully feel it. To embrace it. Venerable Guan Zhen, reminded me that as humans we experience all kinds of emotions. Even monks experience emotions. And it is recognizing these emotions, understanding them, and learning to handle them that is part of our path to enlightenment.

Grief can be a physical reaction. Venerable Guan Zhen described it as a chemical reaction occurring in his body, which was triggered by his shock, sadness, and grief at the news of his father's death. Diane Wilde felt it in her throat. When she told me that, I was so relieved, because I did too. Even now, when I experience moments of grief, it is like my throat is threatening to close right up!

When Timber Hawkeye first experienced grief, it was not caused by death. Grief came to him when his parents disowned him. You see, when Timber was eighteen, he chose to date someone that they did not like. They did not approve, and they expected Timber to obey them. When he did not, they told him that he was dead to them. While he was very much alive, their choice of cutting him off was very painful. He describes it as a feeling of betrayal. This conscious choice to not be in his life led him to grief. Timber points out that when someone dies, they have not betrayed you, they have gone through the natural and inevitable process of dying. Having his parents cut him off was a different form of grief.

In fact, for Timber, the idea of grieving death does not necessarily work for him. He tends to shy away from funerals and public displays of grieving. One of his concerns is that at some point, the gathering stops being about the person who has died and turns into a bit of a pity party—too much about the sorrow of being the one who is left behind. He is much more in favor of life celebrations. Joyfully remembering that your loved one was a part of your life and showing your appreciation for your connection. In this way, it is not about, "Poor me, my loved one is gone." Timber will also be the first one to tell you that others have accused him of being insensitive for not subscribing to societal norms.

Timber's favored approach would involve spending our time and money on visiting our loved ones while we are all still alive, as opposed to traveling great distances to attend the funeral so that other family members can notice that you were there. Be a caring friend or family member when your loved one is alive.

How we experience grief is directly related to the state we are in at the time of our loss. Noël Alumit, Dave Smith, and

Venerable Karma Lekshe Tsomo all shared stories of how death experienced when we are young, or when we do not have the tools or help to cope, can linger for decades, perhaps even an entire lifetime.

Noël looks back on his time doing hospice work during the AIDS pandemic. Even now, each year on World AIDS Day, there is a woman he still remembers. Sometimes he thinks that he did not handle her death well. That perhaps he could have been more engaged with her. Yet he understands that at age twenty-two or twenty-three, he did not have the emotional capacity to deal with all the fear and death that was coming his way. This was a time when AIDS patients were being shunned by their family and friends. Now when he hears about soldiers returning to civilian life after active duty, he feels a deep empathy for the trauma and mental illness that so many of them deal with. Like Venerable De Hong, Noël believes that grief directly impacts your mental health. He does not regret the time he spent being with the dying during the AIDS pandemic, but it has left an indelible mark on his psyche.

Describable and Indescribable

If grief is different from person to person, and from loss to loss, is it possible to describe it to others? Yes, no, and maybe. Most of the people I spoke to were willing to give it a shot. Look at these descriptions, and you might find yourself saying, "Oh yes, that is it." Or you might have your own personal definition.

Diane Wilde said:

"I think I would say it is the experience of the heart being so full that it breaks. It is so full of love and it's full of grief, and it just can't contain anymore, it breaks, and then it comes back together again. That breaking, I think it puts us in touch with all sentient beings, and I now feel much more compassionate, and kind to other beings. It was like my heart finally understood what every living being goes through, and I was just filled with so much compassion, knowing that we are all going to deal with this."

Seth Segall explained grief as a kind of protest or nonacceptance of loss. Someone that we cherished, or who was inextricably bound up with our well-being, is gone. We might find ourselves feeling unsupported, angry, sad, or dead inside. It can be any of these things, or a mixture of these different feelings.

To illustrate his perspective, Seth shares a story of one of his patients. He was seeing this patient weekly, and the patient was severely depressed. During the time he spent in therapy, he had a week that would have been extremely difficult for most of us. During one week, he lost his job and his mother died. Seth was very concerned about the state of his patient. Yet when the patient arrived for his next appointment, he was in good shape. You see, he truly disliked both the job and his mother. Now he felt tremendous freedom. His two biggest burdens had both disappeared. He even felt strong enough to end his therapy a few weeks later.

Another patient lost her son. He had been on life support, and the doctors advised her that the son was brain dead and counseled her to terminate his life support. So she did. Immediately, she was filled with regret. She felt that rather than let him go, she would rather have had him alive, and at home and receiving full-time care. Every day she regretted her decision. She would visit the graveyard and pray that he would come back. After a year of therapy and trying multiple approaches, she was still filled with regret, and visiting the graveyard, praying for her son's return.

The point in considering both of Seth's stories is to examine the contrasts. There is such a variable range of reactions and recoveries. Some people move on right away, while some people may never move on. Most of us are somewhere between those two points. Our healing time is our healing time. While there are many things we share in our grief, it is still a different experience for each of us. Like snowflakes or fingerprints—similar, yet no two are exactly alike.

Perhaps, like Cayce Howe, you might prefer not to put words around it because it is unique to be experienced in our way by each of us. Cayce expressed a strong preference for encouraging others to be with grief, to sit with their grief and to accept how it felt for them.

Additionally, in English, we might not have the proper words to describe the different levels of grief. There is subtle grief, and there is much larger grief. Yet we seem to use one word for both conditions. Therefore, Cayce suggests dropping all the words and trying to be in the experience of it. We do not need to describe it, we just need to feel it—to embrace the process of grief, and the changing and shifting that is occurring within us. To be in grief is to be amid something that is dynamic. There is nothing to be done, other than to just hold the moment. You are sitting with such strong feelings, and in the next moment or moments, those feelings will change.

If grief is different for each of us, and if some of us are hesitant to describe it, is there something—anything—that our spirituals leaders agree on? Perhaps Seth Segall put it best when he said, "I think the first thing is that however you're feeling, that's fine. I mean whatever you're feeling, accept that it's okay to be feeling that way. That there's no way you should or shouldn't be feeling in that moment, and I think being able to just be open to whatever was there and to be with it. And to allow it to be there."

He reminds us that whatever your initial feelings are, they do not have to remain the same forever. This, too, was a common thread among our teachers. With the passing of time your feelings will change, and you will be changed by this experience. Do not expect to go back to a past version of yourself.

On Where You Grieve

Where you grieve can be very important. Especially if you shared a space with your recently deceased. This topic came up when Venerable De and I were discussing our experiences with grief. It seems like there are two distinct paths. One stems from not wanting to stay in the space you shared with your loved one. The second involves not wanting to leave the area you shared with your loved one. Which one is the best and most healthy decision to support you as you grieve? The one that provides you the greatest sense of peace and security and well-being. A caveat to this: if you cannot afford to stay in your current living situation, do not cling to it. This will ultimately cause you more harm than good. If this is the case, find a living situation that supports your emotional and financial needs.

You might be surprised by your choice. I had always believed that when the time came that I was left alone in the house that my husband Ed and I shared, I would leave. I never envisioned that I would want to stay or that I would be able to stay. And yet, as he approached his final days, I went through a shift. I could not imagine leaving a space that was filled with so much love and happy memories. I was able to find a balance, and stay, without turning it into some kind of "Ed and Margaret museum."

Venerable De had shared his home with his mother. After she died, he chose to stay and live by himself. Friends and family members questioned his decision. In fact, this is something that we both experienced. Most of our friends and family members expected us to leave. Or to at least have someone stay with us. At first, it is strange to be alone in a space that you shared with your loved one. You might find it peaceful, or you might find it overwhelming. Be aware of how you are feeling, and act accordingly.

Seek to make your choice from a place of equanimity. If you decide to stay, try not to do so because you are clinging to your old life. That life is gone. I did not change everything right away. Some immediate changes were obvious. The hospice came to pick up the hospital bed and their other equipment. I disposed of unneeded medications and supplements. I did the laundry and sorted out items to be donated. I kept an item or two for myself. Even though I knew that this was a form of clinging, I found it useful to have something that belonged to Ed. I found that I let go of things in phases. And one day, I realized that I wanted to re-landscape the front yard. I wanted to repaint some walls. I wanted to rearrange the dining room. I was making our space into my space. It felt natural and healthy.

If you decide to leave, know that a change of scenery can help escort you into your new life, but it will not alleviate your pain. Your experiences and emotions follow you wherever you go. A new place to live does not stop grief. But, in certain financial and difficult emotional situations, it can be the right choice for you.

On Meditating

Speaking with Diane Wilde was very validating and helpful. In some ways, it made me wish that when I had first met her, I had shared with her my status as a widow. We met at a retreat for volunteers teaching dharma in California State Prisons. I was in my first year on my own. That was not the purpose of the retreat, and I was very private about my grief. Little did I know that she had walked the same path. And because she had walked this path, so much of our discussion was me saying, "Oh, that happened to me too."

One of the biggest *aha* moments I had was when she brought up the topic of meditating while grieving. As much as I sought to practice self-compassion, I was very judgmental of my inability to meditate. I actually thought, "What the hell kind of Buddhist are you, Margaret? You're in your deepest, darkest moment, and you can't use your Buddhism?" Diane came right out and said, "At first, you may not be able to meditate. And when you can, all of your meditations are not going to be epiphanies."

Boom, there it was! There was part of me that thought that I was not a good Buddhist because I was either completely unable to concentrate, or I was unable to mediate without it turning into one gigantic ugly cry. Turns out, it was not that I could not use my Buddhism, it was that I was too fixated on what I perceived to be the right way to meditate.

Diane recalled talking to her teacher, Gil Fronsdal, about her experience. She expressed that when she tried to sit, her grief was overwhelming. Each time she was overcome by images of her husband Larry as he was dying. And all she could focus on was how much she missed him. Instead of giving her concentration techniques, or telling her to just keep sitting, Gil told her that what she needed was to get back into her body. He advised her that right now was not the time to sit. It was the time to walk. It was not that she could not mediate, it was that walking meditation was a better tool for her. So that is what she did. She walked and walked. The walking did not completely remove her pain, but it helped tremendously. And as she began to get back into her body, she was able to experience her grief differently. She was able to investigate it. She became both scientist and experiment. She was able to locate where her grief was in her body.

When Diane told me that she felt her grief in her throat, I had yet another *aha* moment. About a year into my grieving process, I went to a holistic doctor. She asked about what I had been experiencing. I recall mentioning a tightness in my throat. Her reply to me was, "I knew you were going to say that." Unfortunately, she did not elaborate, and I did not ask how she knew. I did not know that this was a common experience. I remember having days where I felt like someone had punched me in the throat. It was that strong.

Through walking meditation, Diane became interested in observing her grief—in feeling it rising and falling. And the more that she was able to watch her grief, the more it seemed to fade. It had less power over her, and it became an interesting phenomenon. It became more livable. Simply another facet of her experience as a human being.

Do not be harsh with yourself. If sitting meditation is too difficult, give walking mediation and movement a try. See what it is like to live in this body that is grieving. You will be able to come back to sitting meditation when the time is right, and you will rebuild your meditation practice.

On Being Prepared

We face grief in whatever shape we are in at the time. I use the analogy of running a marathon. To successfully complete a marathon takes training. Yes, I am like a dog with a bone about the concept of training for death!

Our wise teachers who felt ill-prepared during their first encounters with death and grief can now express what eventually helped them to understand the loss they felt. Venerable Karma Lekshe Tsomo came to see death as a universal process. As her life path led her to Buddhism, she saw that everyone experiences death and grief. She learned that accepting death as part of our shared experience and understanding that there is no getting around it was tremendously helpful. If the adults in her life had been able to discuss death with children, and to teach them that everything—plants, pets, wild animals, and human beings—all have a life cycle, then losing her dog as a child would have been easier. Yes, she still would have been sad—but death would not have seemed like some type of punishment from on high. She reminded me that technically our bodies are arising and perishing from one moment to the next. We are not static or fixed, we are constantly changing. That change is part of impermanence. We are in a sense being born, and dying, over and over throughout the day.

Part of each of our experiences stems from our mental, emotional, and spiritual state. Both Dave Smith and Mary Stancavage identify as being in addiction recovery. This is who they are, and we are fortunate that they openly share their experiences and bring it to their practices. Both were teachers I knew of—I had seen their names, and I had read some of their blog posts or descriptions of classes that they taught. Yet it was not until I started the work for this book that I reached out to each of them. And because of their openness, and the way in which they give of themselves to help others, they both said, independently, and in their own way, "Yes, this is important. I would love to speak with you about death."

Dave expresses it in this way, "It's not so much that I have addiction. It's that I have trauma. Ah, and addiction was my solution or my medication." For several years in his life, Dave leaned on the dharma and his addiction to help him cope. He entertained the notion of giving up the world and becoming a monk. He enjoyed the ability to go on retreat, and while there, he was able to maintain sobriety.

Mary recalls two distinct experiences. When her mother died, Mary was still drinking, and when her brother died, she was sober. This is how Mary describes how she experienced her mother's death:

"I was on the West Coast. She was on the East Coast. I was in college, living with some roommates. When I got home from school, my roommate told me that my brother had called and said that our mother had died. So that was the message, your brother called and said your mom died. And I said, give me a beer because I was not interested in feeling anything."

She goes on to say, "Right, so there is no, there was no investigation of grief and I would get angry at people who said I'm sorry about your mom." Her response was to go right to self-medication.

A few years later, Mary's brother died from cancer. "It was night and day because I was experiencing, that was my first real intimacy experience willingness to be with the feeling of grief, whatever it was to cry in public at the funeral and wake and so it was really interesting." Her ability to be with grief was a welcome experience. This was the experience that she was not ready to have when her mother died. She continued:

"And I also had another interesting experience, the day of my brother's funeral. He was buried in the morning and then that evening we were all sitting around. His wife and children and family out back of their house in New Jersey laughing because we were telling stories. And I remember reflecting, *does this mean I'm not sad?* But then I realized. No, it's just this moment. In this moment, we're just laughing and then the grief would come, and the joy would go and just the movement of the emotions and I realized that, you know, the grief, it's going to come when it comes."

And it did. Sometimes she would be driving down the road, and suddenly, she would think of her brother and burst into tears.

For Mary, acknowledging the grief associated with her parents (who predeceased her brother), occurred while working with her therapist and while deepening her Buddhist practice.

An important lesson that she conveyed to me during our discussion is that just because there is no grieving done, it does not mean there is no grief. The grief is there. Somehow, you have managed to stuff it away. Eventually, it is going to come crawling out of you. Mary really observed this as she developed a formal meditation practice, the things that she had never tended to surface. It was almost as if past experiences would rise to greet her, saying, "Hello, I'm here." In this way, she was able to process the grief that she had tried to stuff away.

Dave and Mary are not the only ones who have balanced trauma, grief, and recovery, while stepping into the dharma. You might be having this experience too. And if not you, perhaps someone you love.

I remember partying with my friends. I know that while I reached a point where I was ready to step away from the party, some of my friends could not. And what had been weekend entertainment for me was a way of covering up the pain of past trauma for others. Life does not stop while you work on your sobriety. You might deal with the death of a loved one while you heal your trauma and live life one step at a time. This is part of your experience with grief.

Please remember that your grief is your own. This is not a time to beat yourself up for the state that you are in. After my mother and my husband died, my aunt used to say to me, "Remember, you are not in your right mind." Initially this annoyed the crap out of me. Mostly because I knew she was right. Be honest with yourself, be aware of your triggers, and seek out the help and support that you need.

Cayce Howe shared a story about a Zen master whose son had died. Initially, he is inconsolable. One of his students becomes distressed—after all, shouldn't this great Zen master be able to overcome grief? The student wants to know why his master is crying. The Zen master informs him that he has lost his son. The student finds this answer to be unsatisfactory. He chastises his master by saying, "Isn't it all an illusion?" To which his master replies, "Yes, but losing a son is the greatest of all illusions."

Chapter 6

This Is Not Easy for Any of Us

Not only is death not easy for us, the way in which some people behave toward the dying can be difficult to observe. As a volunteer during the AIDS pandemic, Noël Alumit witnessed this firsthand. Too many times (one time is too many), he saw how people would turn their backs on AIDS patients. Listening to people try to make illness and death the fault of the dying was much more challenging than watching people die. As he told me about this, I wondered out loud, "Do people still treat the dying as if it is their fault?" Unfortunately, in some instances the answer is yes. For some people, blaming others for their deaths is a coping mechanism. "Oh, he smoked. Well, of course he had lung cancer!" Or "Oh, she was an emergency room nurse? Of course she caught COVID."

It is not easy to listen to others place blame on your dead loved one. You do not have to participate in this type of discussion—take care of yourself first. It is not your responsibility to help everyone else come to terms with death. I am not suggesting that you never help others. I am suggesting that you assess the situation. Use your discernment to recognize where and when to use your strength. One of my teachers has reminded me on more than one occasion, you cannot give what you do not have.

When you are better positioned to do so, send compassion to the person who tried to assign blame for death. What that person is really trying to do is cope. Not everyone is able to participate in the type of training and preparation that is part of your practice. If a reason and a cause can be assigned to death, and if there is a way to make that death someone else's fault, then his or her fears can be put to rest. *Thinking about death can be delayed! Just avoid what the deceased did, and you can cheat death.* This is false logic. Fear is not typically a logic-based emotion. Other people's behaviors and their needs to explain away death will not make sense to you. Just remember, this is not easy for any of us.

Overcoming Regret

Avoiding death does not make it less difficult. I understand the desire to try and forget about death until it arrives for yourself or others. Please consider the benefits of consistency in your practice. Venerable Sumitta encourages us all to be positive and realistic. Your practice will help you come to terms with your life, and to overcome regret—regret over your own past behaviors, and regret over troubles in your relationships. He believes that even ten to fifteen minutes of meditation each day can make a huge difference and bring you much inner peace. Your practice will also give you the capacity to make better decisions in your own life. Better decisions lead to less regret and better relationships.

Your ability to release regret is critical to how you handle the loss of your loved ones, and to your ability to experience your own peaceful death. In more than one discussion, the topic of regret surfaced, and the role of regret in grief and death. Venerable Guan Zhen shared with me the realization that when he was bereft over the loss of his father, he began to understand that this came from feeling regret that he would never again spend time with him.

Venerable De was wonderfully open about the role that regret and trauma played when he lost his father, and then years later, his mother. With his father, there was the regret of having been in a relationship with an abuser. While in some ways his father's death freed him from that abuse, it also introduced him to the trauma that he was carrying with him. Grieving for his father was really wrapped up in the sadness and regret that was such a significant part of that relationship.

Before there is a death, you can work on regret. In the Dhammapada, a collection of sayings attributed to the Buddha, is this verse:

> *Some do not understand*
> *that we must die,*
> *But those who do realize this*
> *settle their quarrels.*
> *(The Buddha, Dhp verse 6)*

I would not have envisioned my father as someone with quarrels to settle. But with an understanding that he would die, my father made sure that I would not wonder about his love for me or about what he really thought of me and my life choices.

On a phone call a few years before his cancer diagnosis, Dad became very serious and told me that he always wanted me to know that he loved me and was proud of me, and that there was nothing I had done that he was upset over. It was an important, difficult, and liberating conversation. Important and difficult because together we were acknowledging out loud that his death would come; liberating because it removed any hint of guilt or thought of parental disapproval. In that phone call, Dad made sure I did not have to wonder about his support for me. And that was quite a gift. After he passed, my mother and I built a very rewarding friendship. During that time, we were able to release any hard feelings or misunderstandings that we harbored. Dad, Mom, Ed, and I were fortunate to be able to let go of regret. This is not always the case.

Diane Wilde, Venerable De, and I have all spent time sharing Buddhism in the California State Prison system. Diane and Venerable De have spent much more time than I have. We all have heard incarcerated men and women express sadness over broken relationships. We have seen them cry at the idea of losing a parent or friend without being able to work through hard feelings, or say, "I am sorry." This is not just true for the incarcerated. There will be people with whom you lose touch, or who you think you have more time with, or you are not able to move forward with. When this occurs, treat yourself with loving kindness, and when you are ready, include him or her in your *metta* practice too. Consider writing a letter with what you wanted to say, and then read it out loud. You can still work on releasing your regret and move yourself to a place of peace with your past relationships.

Have an Open Heart

Working with others who are grieving has taught me an important lesson. Not only is this difficult for all of us, but there are also different degrees of difficulty and suffering. Others have experiences that are completely different from yours. I will admit, there has been a time or two where I realized that I was being judgmental about the way in which someone was navigating their grief. There was this part of me that just knew how they should act, what they needed to hear, and more. Or I would look at someone and think, "Yes, it sucks that your dog died, but you *should* be able to get up and leave your house and go to work." But one day it hit me—I was beginning to act in a way that I found objectionable when I was grieving. When people would come to me and tell me what I should be doing, or how I should be acting. And it really annoyed me. How embarrassing, but at the same time, what an amazing lesson in compassion and understanding the suffering of others.

It does not matter if I think you should be able to get up and go to work the day after your dog died. It does not matter if I think you should be able to pull it together and go to the grocery store by yourself. What matters is that you are suffering, and it is not my role to judge what is acceptable suffering. To be helpful, I need to simply understand that you are suffering—and to be compassionate is to see your suffering—and wish to alleviate your suffering and act when I can. Sometimes, the most compassionate thing I can do is to send you *metta*. With this realization came another component to my death training plan—a reminder that just because I have walked through an experience does not mean I am an expert or stronger or doing a better job. We are not all running the exact same race, so let's just support one another's experiences.

Venerable Karma Lekshe Tsomo wisely said to me, "I think the important thing is for us to have an open heart. To have an open heart to meet each person wherever they may be, we have a tendency to want to change others. The only person we can really change is ourself. But often by intending to transform others we do them injustice."

In starting these discussions with our twelve wise teachers, I wondered if I was going to learn the secret to dealing with death. Probably one of our wise teachers would tell me how to make this easy, or share with me that now, it was easy for him or her. But that's not what happened. In a group of people with a collective hundreds of years of spiritual practice, not one of them said, "Oh, Margaret, this is easy, here is the secret." Or "Oh, Margaret, this is easy, there is a secret, but I cannot tell you."

We had excellent discussion about how to make death less painful, alleviate suffering, and take care of ourselves. But there was never a promise that grief would simply go away. This is not easy for any of us. Keep practicing and training yourself, and when grief arises, follow the advice of Venerable Karma Lekshe Tsomo—keep an open heart, and meet yourself wherever you may be.

Chapter 7

Impermanence and Attachment

Please do not think that to be a good Buddhist means that you are already beyond suffering. Most of us are who are practicing have not reached enlightenment. Some people may not understand this. I know that recently I overheard a member of a local meditation group chastise another by saying, "I thought you were a meditator, you should be able to withstand this. Maybe you are not doing it right." Ouch, that is some very human judgment in action.

You will experience impermanence in all aspects of your life, every day. Sometimes more than once a day. When Dave Smith and I were discussing this, he wisely reminded me that in every moment there is a death. Not just the big death. He pointed out that when we ended our Zoom session, we would both click off and the session would die. But later the session would experience rebirth, as a book and as a podcast. Rising and ceasing, we are going to lose it all—pets, friends, and family members. And when we do, sadness is an appropriate emotional response. If you want to transcend sadness, then learn how to be sad. Your Buddhist practice is the vehicle that allows you to work with all of this. Or as Dave stated, ". . . you can explore all the tricky bizarre scary beautiful territories of the human experience."

On Love and Attachment

"It is that someone that we cherished and who cherished us and has seemed to be inextricably bound up with our well-being is gone. So we've lost like a major source and support for ourselves. It can feel like anger, or sadness, or even deadness. It could be like anything, each of us are very individual and those different feelings mix together... you'll never be the same again in the way that you were before, because we never were. We were always being changed by experiences from then on, it's a different life. That's the other Buddhist teaching of impermanence and always being reborn," Seth Segall observed.

As I review his words, the phrase, "inextricably bound up," really jumps out at me. That's attachment. The feeling that our relationship with our loved one is part of our security, a part of what makes us OK. It's why when someone you love dies, you feel insecure. Or why when you contemplate the death of your closest friends and family members, you ponder whether you can survive in a world without them. It is not wrong to love others. It is wise to minimize the clinging in our relationships.

Love without attachment is possible. Attachment is not the same thing as detachment. You care, but it is about how you care. Love using the *Brahma-vihāras*. *Mettā* or loving kindness, *karuṇā* or compassion, *mudita* or sympathetic joy, and *upekkhā* or equanimity. Loving-kindness guards against compassion becoming partiality and prevents it from being discriminating. Loving-kindness gives equanimity its selflessness. Compassion prevents love and sympathetic joy from forgetting that there is also suffering. Compassion prevents complacency and stops equanimity from becoming cold and indifferent. Sympathetic joy keeps compassion from being overwhelmed by the suffering. Sympathetic joy also helps ward off envy.

Equanimity is the result of the other three and stabilizes or reinforces them. Compassion without equanimity can result in overwhelming sadness and an inability to contemplate the suffering of others repeatedly. Equanimity provides balance and the ability to contemplate the suffering of others with a more dispassionate nature. When the *Brahma-vihāras* are used in meditation, they can lead to a pure state of mind. When they are used to love others, they can lead to a love that is free from clinging. Cayce Howe once shared an example of what it means to love without attachment. He said it meant that if your partner called you from Mexico and said, "I'm not coming home, I have found the love of my life, and we are staying here together," you can take that phone call, be happy for your partner, and sincerely wish him or her good things and happiness. Imagine being that accepting. That is really a love without attachment and a strong understanding of impermanence.

Impermanence Is Fun (No Really)

Sometimes we forget that we are always changing. Many days the changes we experience are imperceptible. Maybe a new freckle pops up, a new gray hair sprouts, a wrinkle deepens, or we gain or lose a few pounds. But if we take a photo at the beginning of the year, and then compare it to another photo at the end of the year, some of these changes become noticeable. Seth is right—we are always being changed. We just are not always noticing. If we let it, awareness of the moment-to-moment, day-to-day elements of impermanence help pave the way for the larger and more obvious changes.

Timber Hawkeye introduced me to an attitude toward impermanence that was adventurous and fun. He told me, "The only thing I know for certain, is that I don't know anything for certain. So why would I put so much faith in that, as opposed to whatever the great unknown has directed my life so far and always provided, and kept me here for as long as it has? It clearly knows more than I do."

In that moment, he reminded me of an aspect of Buddhism that was so refreshing to me. In my "other" life, the life where I am not sharing Death Dhamma, I teach project management. I teach people how to plan and schedule things. And yet, as I became a Buddhist, one of the things that was the most refreshing to me was not having to know the answers.

There was planning and scheduling that took place to have all of these insightful discussions. I wanted them to go as planned. I wanted to talk to people and learn from them, and move forward with *The Death Dhamma Podcast* and with this book. There was also the possibility that we would need to reschedule, or that the internet would crash. And while we had good internet karma for our discussions, there were reschedules. Any one of us could have become frustrated and attached to the idea of a specific interview occurring on a specific day. The result of that attachment would be some self-inflicted suffering. The solution is not to live without any plan or intention. Have a plan and be open to the changes that will come your way.

Resistance to impermanence causes suffering. Timber has an equation that really puts it into perspective,

"Pain + Resistance = Suffering."

What if we worked on being more open, and developed an understanding that no matter what happens, we will be OK? That does not mean that difficulties will not come. It means you must accept that difficulty will come, and that you can handle those difficulties. The analogy that Timber provided was that tomorrow he could be in an accident, which could change his physical or mental abilities. That does not mean he is not well—

it means that he needs to change his view of what it means to be well, and to let go of clinging to the Timber who existed before the accident.

His comments really resonated with me. I remember in the early stages of my grief knowing that this was difficult, but that I was going to be OK, and that being OK did not mean that my dead family members were going to resurrect themselves. It meant that I was going to resurrect myself. Or to use more Buddhist friendly terms, they had their rebirth, and in this life, I was going to have mine.

No Blame, No Shame

None of this is to place blame on any of us. Timber gently stated that we may unconsciously be clinging to something, or unaware that we're doing it. He feels that Buddhism helps to hold a mirror up to us, to show us what we are doing to ourselves. There staring us in the face is the suffering we have created through our own attachments.

Another facet that comes with clinging is wanting to know what will happen. Being uncomfortable with uncertainty. With death, there is one certainty—we will all die. The rest may be a complete surprise. Uncertainty is difficult; perhaps we do not want to know when our exact moment of death will arise, but we want to know what it will be like. We like to bargain with it. I know I like the idea of being able to die peacefully in my sleep. I can wish for that, but I cannot plan for it.

Venerable Karma Lekshe Tsomo taught me that we can look directly at our grief. And because all things are impermanent, we can develop the understanding that our grief is also impermanent. As we look directly into our grief, it will begin to dissolve. It will start to disentangle and lose its grip on our hearts. And the pain and tightness that comes with grief, well, it too will begin to dissolve. This will take time—it is not going to happen overnight. We need to continue to be dedicated to our practice, and to include staring our grief in the face as part of our regular practice.

Let's Keep Learning

Venerable Sumitta taught his own mother about impermanence and death. His role as a Buddhist monk made him the one that his family turned to for emotional and spiritual support. Over the years, advancing in his own education and practice required him to move away from his home in Sri Lanka. He spent time in India and eventually came to the United States. I had the good fortune (or good karma) to meet him at University of the West in Southern California, and to visit the Sri Lankan temple where he teaches the dharma. While she appreciated the work that her son was doing, his mother missed him greatly. And like most mothers she wanted to keep in touch with him on a regular basis. She expressed the desire for him to call her at least once a week. He said to her, "Do not expect me to call you on a regular schedule. Like I call every Saturday at a specific time or something. If you expect that, that will create a negative attachment. I will call you occasionally, but it should not be regular. And you should not expect to call me all the time either. I don't want this type of attachment to happen to you."

What a difficult lesson for a mother to learn. The very nature of the mother/child relationship is attachment. Without that early attachment, the child would not survive. He worked to free her from attachment to all her children, and to become prepared for her own death. He would remind her that she had already lost a husband, daughter, and son. He would tell her, "No, you are free, you should not be attached to your children or property or anything. Just relax, be free. Go to the temple. You do whatever you want but relax and don't get attached to anything or anyone anymore. And be ready because you know that your day is coming. It will come to us all, as you know, my sister has died, and my brother has died. And so naturally you will too, you should be ready for that."

As they aged, my parents did an excellent job of reminding me that one day they would be gone. They approached it from a practical perspective, advising me of where things were, and what to do, and who to call. Together we acknowledged that it would be very difficult to say goodbye. I do not know that I would have been able to take the lead in the discussion, and to teach them to prepare for their own impermanence.

In having these discussions, I really thought that I was solid in my recognition of impermanence. Then Noël Alumit told me about a Japanese Buddhist funeral that he attended. The Zen priest reminded the attendees that everything passes—*even Buddhism*.

Boom, drop the mic. In my attachment to being a Buddhist and discussing death through the lens of Buddhism with Buddhist teachers, never had I allowed myself to consider that even Buddhism is impermanent. Today, I am a Buddhist. Tomorrow, maybe there will be no Buddhism—maybe I will be something else, or nothing else.

Chapter 8

Grief Has No Schedule

Ok, you say, *I get it*. Dealing with death and dying and grief is not easy for any of us. But if I have suffering, I am not a bad Buddhist. In fact, all Buddhists will experience death and loss. All of us will experience impermanence. Each time we do, it will be different, and with different degrees of difficulty, running the gamut of emotions.

Still, you wonder, *How long is this going to take? When will I be fully trained, and ready to cross the finish line?* I say, "I don't know. It takes what it takes." You may find that many of the people around you expect you to be "over it" in three to six months. Usually, these are people who have either not yet gone through an intensive grieving process, or possibly, they come from a place of cutting off their emotions. They have never allowed themselves to fully feel their grief. Someone who has fully participated in grieving learns not to put timelines and expectations on themselves or others.

Two years after seeing his wife through her death from cancer, Seth Segall remarried. Some people did not think he had grieved for enough time. There were people who did not understand and were critical of his decision. He was accused of being unfeeling. But if you ever heard him talk about his first wife, and their time together, you would know that there was a tremendous love. He had a full acceptance of his loss, and although he grieved her, he understood that he was still alive.

In many ways there is no win. I am writing this at a point where I have been a widow for seven years. I know that I have some friends who expect me to be on my own forever, and I have some friends who are less than subtle in their reminders that the clock is ticking. I do my best to ignore all opinions. My life will unfold as it unfolds. Seth's opinion is that other people cannot know your timeline, your emotional state, or what is right for you.

Mary Stancavage told me, "There's no timeline, no time. I still come up with some grief around my father's death and we're talking sixty years." After nine years, Venerable Guan Zhen still misses his father. He believes that a part of us will always miss the ones who die before us.

He still remembers the difficulty he had during the first six months after his father died. Even up to one year after, every time he thought of his father, his thoughts turned to the things he wanted to be able to tell him, and the sadness from not seeing him one more time. As we spoke, I shared the concept that time is our difficulty, but it is also our friend. Time is our difficulty when we are still close to the day of the death, and as it passes and our grief changes, time becomes our friend. Venerable Guan Zhen then reminded me that time is just time, it is how we deal with our emotions over the passing of time that makes the difference.

A good friend told me that the first year of grieving was hard, but that the second year was even more difficult. I was so annoyed. I really wanted to tell her to shut up. I restrained myself. On some level, I knew she was trying to be helpful. In my second year of grieving my mother and husband, I did see the truth in her words. For me, it was like I had made it through an entire year of events and anniversaries and birthdays. Naively, I thought they would not be difficult next time. When those events came around again, it was like a slap in the face. "Oh, you're back? And it still hurts. And I am still experiencing some attachment."

I have a friend who has been a widow for three years, and she still is not comfortable going to any kind of celebratory event. There is part of me that wants her to be able to move forward, and there is another part of me that recognizes that she feels what she feels. And although it hurts my heart that she does not believe she can be happy, who I am to tell her what to do and how to feel?

One of the most important lessons for you when it comes to grief is that it takes more time than you think. In fact, it's best not to think of it in terms of a timetable, or as something to get through. I have come to think of grief as just one of many emotions that come with being human. The possibility for grief to arise exists. Just as the potential for anger or regret or joy to surface also exists. You will have longer periods between visits from grief, but it may surface at any time. I recall walking into the bakery section of a grocery store, seeing lemon cupcakes, and before I knew it, tears started streaming down my face. This was two years after my mother had died. And yes, she was a fan of lemony baked goods.

When grief or sadness comes, greet it. Notice it, sit with it, walk with it, feel it. Observing your grief changes how it impacts you.

Eventually you will go from feeling sharp stabbing pains of sadness to a dull ache, and one day, quiet joy. There is a popular analogy that is used to explain grief. It is called the ball and the box. The first time I saw it, I wished I had thought of it. Then I realized that was my ego trying to take over. Now I am just glad the analogy exists. It goes like this:

Imagine your life is a box, and grief is a ball inside that box. Inside that box there is a pain button. When your loss is new, the grief ball is so big that every time you move, the grief ball hits the pain button. In other words, just getting through your day is extremely painful. That grief ball is bouncing around in the box, constantly hitting your pain button. As you continue with your life, the ball begins to shrink. It still moves around in the box, but as the ball gets smaller, it does not always hit the pain button. Sometimes the ball bounces around and does not hit the pain button, but sometimes it does. And it hurts, and grief wells up within you. But over time, the ball keeps shrinking, and that means there could be long of periods where it never hits the pain button. But the ball is never completely gone, and sooner or later, it will hit the pain button. This may surprise you because it has not happened for quite some time. When it hits the pain button, it will bring back your grief. You do not get rid of grief; it changes. But you learn to live with the ball and the pain button.

(Source: *psychcentral.com/blog/coping-with-grief-the-ball-the-box#1*)

There will be a time when you will think of your deceased loved one, and while you will still miss him or her, your memories will bring a smile to your face.

Chapter 9

Talking to Dead People

I have a confession to make: I still talk to my dead people. I used to hide this, I used to feel guilty about it, but I no longer feel that is necessary. Now I understand that I am in good company. The topic of speaking to our dead friends and family members came up in discussions with Noël Alumit, Holly Hisamoto, Venerable De Hong, Venerable Sumitta, Diane Wilde, and Venerable Guan Zhen. I am not going to question their collective wisdom, but I will breathe a sigh of relief, and you should too. Not only is it OK to talk to your dead friends and family members, but it can also be helpful.

Wonderful and Unexplainable

Diane Wilde recounts how she will call on her deceased husband Larry to help her find her keys. In life, they had some great balance. She could lose anything and he could find it. And now, she will silently ask for his help, and *most* of the time it works. She does not know whether it is Larry or some other type of consciousness, but it helps.

My father used to have an amazing ability to find a parking space. He would confidently drive into a full parking lot and find the one open spot. It would be a good parking spot too—just the right size, and close to our destination. One day, after his death, in a parking-challenged situation, I called out, "Dad, could you please help me find a parking space." And it worked! Now, I encourage my friends to call out to my dad when they cannot find parking. I have one friend who swears it helps her on a regular basis.

Diane phrased it in such an upbeat manner, "I think there's just wonderful unexplainable things that happen. In 1998, we were having a memorial service for my father. We're sitting in the living room and the phone started making the weirdest noises I have ever heard—it was ringing and doing these weird things. I picked it up and there was static on it. When I would hang it up, it all started again. My husband said, 'It's your dad.' I somehow believe it probably was. I don't know how but it never happened again—the phone was fine after that day."

Diane also brought up the subject of dreams, and how a friend of hers who is a Zen priest helped her understand that dreams are another way in which we maintain a connection with our deceased. After her husband died, Diane had many vivid dreams of him. One of these dreams involved her having a discussion with Larry, and he said to her, "I have to talk quickly because soon I will fade out." He wanted her to know that he was great, and he thought that she was going to be OK and was doing a terrific job in handling herself. Then, he did start to fade away, and that was the end of the dream.

Finding Joy

Holly Hisamoto is a woman who really has a handle on having a balanced relationship with her deceased, especially her sister. Holly will tell you that her relationship with her sister after her death has taught her that tragic deaths can be our teachers.

Holly's younger sister Maya died at the age of twenty-three. It was a sudden and unexpected death. Holly and Maya had been extremely close. Holly was left navigating shock and existential anger and sorrow and multifaceted grief. And the person who would have helped her through this was gone. With the passing of time, Holly has learned to celebrate Maya and the great qualities that she had. To find joy in that she was able to have Maya in her life at all, and to honor some of the qualities that Holly possesses that came from her relationship with Maya.

"So, for example, I tend to be kind of serious, and most people think of me as serious, but me and my sister were very goofy together, and had an ironic sense of humor and there's just parts of my personality that I developed because of her." She attributes humor, playfulness, and the unconditional support that she offers her loved ones as gifts from her sister. These attributes are blessings that she received.

As part of her own practice, Holly will write letters to her sister. These might be updates about her life, or feelings and situations that she is navigating. She also acknowledges that her ability to be in a relationship with Maya has changed with the passing of time and the shifting of her grief. Sometimes you might reject the thing you bonded over. With Holly and her father, this was music. Right after her father died, she could not listen to music. Her grief was too new—too raw—and music brought her sadness. Then one day, she was able to listen a little bit, but with a lot of melancholy. Eventually, she could listen with openness and a more joyful remembrance of her father. But even then, there could be times when hearing a specific song could bring her to tears.

The Case of the Lemon Cupcakes

"Why don't you make your lemon cupcakes again? They were a hit last time." I had no idea what my friend was saying. I understood that she was giving me suggestions about what to bring to an event we were attending, but the lemon part was wrong. She must have had me confused with someone else.

Seeing the puzzled look on my face, she said, "Don't you remember, last year you brought a tray of lemon cupcakes, and they disappeared as soon as you put them on the dessert table?" Then it clicked—I had brought lemon cupcakes to the party. Over the previous year, I had brought lemon cupcakes or lemon cookies to more than one event. And with that realization came another—I was making the things that my mother used to bake. In the year after her death, I had been visited by her baking spirit. I unconsciously started to cook like Mom. My choices were particularly ironic as her love of citrus and spice and caramel had always baffled me. Those things were all fine, but I could not understand why anyone would choose those flavors instead of chocolate.

An inspection of my freezer revealed that my favorite chocolate chip mint ice cream had been replaced by dulce de leche and pralines and cream—Mom's two favorite ice cream flavors. I was the only one buying the ice cream, and these were my selections. It was quite a shock when I began to understand how I unknowingly was adopting Mom's preferences. After the shock wore off, I began to embrace the opportunities to bake something that Mom would have baked, cook a meal that she would have cooked, or visit a restaurant that she would have liked. It was my way of honoring her memory and continuing my relationship with her.

Even if you do not talk to your dead people, you are still influenced by them. In addition to baking lemony treats, I also carried my mother's etiquette around with me. My mother was a very proper woman. I think she might have been happier in the Victorian era. She was ready to have tea with the queen at any moment. One of her favorite expressions was, "No matter how painful, be a lady." As I became older and more sassy, I would retort, "Oh, it is killing me." Now there are times where I have said to friends, "If I do that, my mother will reassemble her ashes, and come back and smack me for my lack of manners." Most people laugh. One or two people have said something along the lines of, "Well, that was very graphic." Or "Margaret, I think you have a problem." Yes, I have a problem or two or three, but remembering my mother and her code of etiquette is not one of them.

May Your Merit Find Them

Venerable Sumitta mentions that sometimes he can close his eyes and feel like his deceased mother is still present and in Sri Lanka. When he does this, he feels even closer to her—almost as if his mother is right in front of him. Or perhaps when the wind blows, he feels a little bit like his mother is passing by.

His experience and his description of it helped ease my mind. I explained to him that there are absolutely times when I feel like some of my dead family members are with me. But then, I feel guilty. I think that I should not want them to be with me, because they should have moved on. They should be in their next rebirth, not here with me. I should not even want them to be in their next rebirth, the goal that I wish for them is *nibbana*. If I close my eyes and feel like they are with me, is that really them? Or is it that in that moment something has triggered a memory of them? Venerable Sumitta told me that it could be either. Perhaps some do stay around us. What we can do to honor and respect our deceased is to engage in good actions.

Those of us who are still here can help our dead ones by generating merit, and by dedicating that merit to them. We generate merit by performing good deeds with pure intention and acting honorably. We cannot do anything about the fact that they have died. We cannot control if they are reborn, or when or where they are reborn. We can send them merit, and if the conditions are right, your merit will benefit them. When you are able to channel the energy of your grief into doing good deeds for others, or sending your compassionate thoughts to others, you are creating positive energy, and the deceased may benefit from that energy. In this way you can acknowledge that they are gone, and without attachment, keep them in your heart, and do good things in their name. Again, if the conditions are right, the merit you generate on their behalf may find them.

You Have a Team

"Now they are on Team Noël." This is how Noël Alumit described his departed friends and family. He describes having conversations with his dead father, and others, as an important part of his spiritual practice. He would say to his father, "Okay, Dad, I really need help with Mom right now," when he was seeking advice on how to help his mother through a difficult situation she was facing. Noël wanted to tap into his father's wisdom. He points out that your discussions do not just have to be with deceased family members. You can talk to anyone you admired or thought of as a mentor while they were alive. Now they are your ancestors, and they are part of your team. If lots of people in your life have passed, then guess what? You have a really big team!

In these discussions with our wise teachers, I began to feel like I was maybe starting to understand the concept of ancestor veneration. Having grown up in the United States, in a Caucasian Christian family, I really did not understand the practice of worshipping our ancestors. When Noël talked about his dead friends and family being on his team, or when Venerable De Hong mentioned the ceremonies he and his siblings conducted for their mother. I began to have a glimpse of the power of ancestor veneration. It really began to crystallize for me when I was speaking with Venerable Guan Zhen.

For me, the idea of an altar had a very specific association with a church, God, and a priest leading us through a worship service. The altar was something we saw during a service, but only a few special individuals could actually be on the altar. My Buddhist teachers have shown me that an altar dedicated to their deceased father or mother is not the same thing. I misunderstood veneration as worship. It is not worship, it is remembrance and respect. It is a way of keeping a family member with you, and when incorporated with Buddhism, it is a balanced and nonattached memorial. Venerable Guan Zhen told me, "In Buddhism, to have the ancestors there is to remind yourself how much love you have received, and have access to, and also to, you know, to look at as an example for you to live on." An altar to your father reminds you of the good deeds of your father, the love you received from him, and the love you still feel for him. It is also a reminder to learn from his example. Your ancestors are your teachers. In other words, they are on your team.

When someone you love dies, you will still think of them, and you will talk to them. You may have dreams about them or moments when you think you hear their voice, or even believe that you see them across the room. If your email server goes crazy, you might start receiving emails from them. One day, several months after my godfather died, my inbox became full of the many joke emails he used to send. It took me more than a few minutes to catch my breath and see that the emails dated from before his death.

It's Not About Clinging

Don't get me wrong here—I am not encouraging an unhealthy attachment to your dearly departed. As you follow your grief through its natural progression, your discussions will become less frequent. Talk to them—it is a way of acknowledging the bond you had. It is a way of honoring that they are a part of you, and that while they were alive, you were a part of them. You do not need to throw any of that away. You still have a relationship, it has just changed. I have to come to think of it in this way, if I am in fact creating these instances where I think my father is telling me something, or my husband is sending me a message, perhaps it is the way in which my subconscious and intuition are advising me that something is important.

This is about honoring your relationship with your dead loved ones. Other people may not understand it, but that is OK. It is between you and your deceased. Just as all relationships change over time, how you will interact with your deceased loved ones will change. You may think about them less often. You might stop speaking to them. But they will always be with you. You will find your way to remember them and honor their memory. Be honest with yourself, are you fully aware that you are finding a way to remember your deceased, or do you think they are still alive? Use your equanimity to balance clinging versus keeping someone in your heart. If you are not sure, talk with a respected Buddhist teacher or your therapist.

Chapter 10

It's Not About Cutting Off Feelings

In our discussion, Venerable Guan Zhen reminded me of something that one of his masters said to him, "Only a stone has no feelings." It should not surprise you that the teachers who spoke to me had strong emotions when their loved ones died. They are only human. Yet each of us has encountered expectations from others who wanted us not to show emotion or acknowledge our feelings. This is not the goal. Buddhist practice is not about cutting off your feelings, it is about meeting them. When feelings arise, do not try to turn them off. Over and over again, the discussions I had with others would eventually land on the importance of being with your feelings, noticing how grief feels in your body, and how sadness and regret and joy can all come to you within the same meditation. One of the best ways to support yourself is to develop an acceptance for sadness and grief. Most of us do not want to have difficult emotions or even acknowledge them—we want to be happy. Remember, you are not training to become devoid of emotions, you are training to recognize your emotions, sit with them, and develop equanimity.

Just Be Happy

When my mother was grieving my father, she turned to her parish priest for guidance. Each time he would say to her, "Just be happy, Joanne. Your husband is where he is supposed to be—be happy." This did little to comfort her. In fact, when she broached the subject with me, she was carrying guilt because she could not be happy, and she was still tremendously sad. The good news is that she sought out the counsel of another priest, one who was able to share more insight with her about the grieving process. One who encouraged her to feel the sadness, allow for moments of joy, and know that she would experience an entire battery of emotions. There was nothing to feel guilty about.

Dave Smith brought up the concept of spiritual bypass. He voiced a concern that some Buddhists he encounters in the United States think that Buddhism is going to help them avoid all of their difficult feelings—that being enlightened means being like a stone. It is as if there is some type of war on suffering. To be released from your suffering does not include declaring war on your most difficult emotions.

I have seen this too. I can think of one or two individuals, who in discussion with other members of our meditation group, will tell people that they need to cut off their feelings—that the moment any emotion arises, the correct response is just to cut it off. Fortunately, our lead teacher will gently break in and suggest a different approach. Reminding all of us that the answer is not to cut off feelings, it is to have the feeling, greet it, and inwardly say, "Oh hello, regret, what will you teach me today?"

Venerable Sumitta has also encountered this aversion to death and a preference for avoiding discussing difficult emotions. He shared a story of a talk he once gave to a delegation from France. As part of the talk, he brought up the topic of death—a reminder that we will all pass. When the talk was over, one of the representatives approached him and admonished him for mentioning death. He advised Venerable Sumitta that "we" do not talk about things like that. It was this and some other experiences that showed him that in much of Western society, there is a preference to hide death and to shy away from discussing our own impermanence. His opinion is that if you ignore death, when it is time to face it, you will be in serious trouble. You will cause yourself panic and distress. If you are ready, you can confidently face the deaths of your loved ones and yourself.

For me, the only way out of the sadness and grief was to go through it. To be with it. To embrace the lessons I had learned in my Buddhist practice. To see my own suffering and attachment, and to offer myself compassion.

If I were to try to define how I regained my strength, I would say that this was the formula:

Time + Self-Compassion + Self-Awareness + Acceptance + Action + Spiritual Path = Strength

Time because, as annoying as it is, it is also true that time can heal all wounds. How much time? That is different for each of us.

Self-Compassion because this is not the time to beat yourself up. I learned to be my own best friend. I did not shirk my responsibilities or engage in harmful behavior. I did treat myself in ways that helped me overcome my grief.

Self-Awareness because I really needed to understand my limitations and boundaries, and then know when to push myself to exceed those limitations.

Acceptance—understanding that my life was changed, but I was still alive.

Action—I did not just sit on my meditation cushion. I got back to work and created a new routine and actively sought to create a new life.

Spiritual Path because I needed meaning and a way to process my grief. In my specific case, Buddhism, the Four Noble Truths, and the Noble Eightfold Path helped me recognize and reflect on my pain.

Like my mother before me, the answer was not to just be happy. The answer was to be with your emotions and be open to your experience.

You Are Not Your Emotions

To acknowledge and be with your emotions does not mean that you become those emotions. This is an important distinction, especially for those who come from a place of just cutting off anything that causes discomfort. Mary Stancavage was spot on when she observed that just because you notice anger arising, it does not mean you have to become angry. Just see that anger is here. She also pointed out that dealing with these feelings is never as bad as we think it is going to be. We are often so afraid of the experience, assuming that we will not be able to survive the losses of friends and family.

Mary's advice is, "Be open to grief. You do not have to jump in 100% right away. You can put your toe in the water, and if you need to step back, then step back. Being compassionate toward your experience is very important as you face this. You do not need to put the pressure on yourself of feeling you have to strive to achieve total oneness with grief." Instead, she suggests understanding the ways in which you have armored yourself. If you first experience loss as a child, you probably had no clue how to handle it. Possibly, you ran away from loss, and your elders in their attempt to protect you may have encouraged denial. If this is true, now is the time for you to chip away at that armor.

"You can be true and vulnerable and open to whatever shows up—whatever experience comes to your undefended heart. We don't have to protect ourselves we can actually be honorable. Because that's where connection and belonging come from, which is how we get through grief. This is what allows us to be connected with others."

We cannot be true and vulnerable, and have an undefended heart, if we have cut off our emotions.

All Feelings Are Welcome

Seth Segall encourages us to be in complete acceptance of our feelings. He says, "The first thing is that however you are feeling, that's fine. Accept that it is OK to be feeling that way. There's no way you should or shouldn't be feeling in that moment... I think is the most important thing. And then I think the second most important thing is to allow whatever those feelings are to change. They don't have to remain the same forever. There's a way in which they open up and change."

Please notice the importance of accepting the impermanence of your feelings. Your healing is not just about noticing and welcoming the difficult emotions, it is also about watching those emotions change and mutate into something else. You are not stuck in one place. It can be easy to grab on to feeling a certain way, and to try to *be* that feeling—to own it or make it part of your personality. I can think of two friends who have fully incorporated the role of *sadness* into their persona. One of them says on a regular basis, "I should be unhappy." Or "This is my time to be unhappy. I cannot be happy." The other friend speaks and behaves in a way that lets us all know that every aspect of her life is difficult, and every day is unbearable. I am not discounting either of their experiences, because losing someone you love can feel insurmountable. I am concerned that by going all-in on sadness or difficulty, each of them is missing the opportunity to notice that their lives are changing.

Seth also said, "You need to give your feelings time. Whether it is a few months or years, one of these is not right and one of them is not wrong." He has seen some miraculous changes in his patients. There was a father whose ten-year-old son died. Every day this man was faced with unremitting grief. When asked if he still felt a connection to his son, perhaps imagining his son in heaven, the father said he had no sense of connection. He did not feel any ability to sense or communicate with his deceased son. He described his experience as having a hole that was right in the center of his being. Then one day, after several months, he described the hole as a tunnel. And in some way, he was able to go into that tunnel, and in that tunnel, he found a connection with his son. This transformation was what allowed him to move on. His gaping hole became the tunnel through which he connected with his grief and his son.

Another patient also experienced her loss as a hole. In this case, it was not in her core, it was next to her. She was able to see it and sit next to it. She meditated next to the hole. Eventually she found herself visualizing filling the hole with rainwater. Then she began to envision plants growing around it. I guess you can say it turned into her grief garden.

The story of the grief garden ties in with an analogy that Dave Smith shared:

"You know, it's about, like, you know, when you're planting a garden. What's the most important part of the garden is that stinky chicken poop nasty fertilizer. You're suffering is your soil. If you plant a tomato seed in beautiful clean sand, or stinky nasty chicken poop fertilizer, where is it going to grow the best?

"We need to be willing to work in that nasty manure. When you work with your hands in the manure, that is the work that leads to the blooms. The nastier the manure, the better the fruit. If you have had lots of suffering, then you've really had the opportunity to blossom in the dharma. Sometimes you are going to be a mess. It is OK to stop worrying about what it means to be a good Buddhist, and just be a mess. And be happy to be messy. On any given day, any one of us is going to be messy. That is part of the process, and part of the lesson. We need to be with our own messiness."

Chapter 11

Accepting Sadness and Joy

We make up our definitions of happy versus unhappy experiences. And when we do, we draw on cultural norms, our own biases, plus our cravings, aversions, and attachments. Then we mix this together and decide how we are supposed to feel. If you win the lottery, you might find one of these to be acceptable responses: joy, happiness, gratitude, or relief. If you feel unhappy or sad, your friends and family might find your response to be unusual. Sometimes we create standards that are too regimented. Previously, I mentioned a friend who has decided that right now, she must be sad. While that is her overarching theme, there have been plenty of times during her declared "time of sadness" that I have heard her laugh and express gratitude and appreciation. I think we have had outings where we had fun. Either she is an amazing actress, or she is experiencing more than sadness.

Most of us have a range of emotional experiences that rise and fall throughout the day. If you are in the midst of grieving, perhaps you assume that you feel nothing but sorrow for twenty-four hours each day. You might feel pressured for this to be true. Pay attention—many emotions will visit you.

Dave Smith has found that his ability to accept and embrace the tragedy that has come his way is directly correlated to his ability to allow joy and happiness into his life. What he shared with me was that we need to be open to all the feelings. We do not get to allow ourselves to only dwell in the positive. We cannot live the dharma and selectively numb ourselves to the negative.

Today I Will Be Happy and Sad and ...

Within sadness is an element of joy. Life is both tragic and beautiful. Most of us will have times when we are in the tragedy of life, while other times we will be in the beauty of life. Dave calls it, "the gestalt of the dharma." It reminds him of those games we see online, where you are asked to look at an image and describe what you see. Some people will see an old woman, others see a beautiful young princess. It is all about how we look at it—both the picture and our lives.

We might tend to think that joyfulness is better than sadness. That is a very conventional human perspective. Let's be happy all the time. Buddhism teaches us to embrace all emotions, at the same level, no matter how we perceive each emotion. The concept of causes and conditions remind us that there will be difficulty and loss. When there is difficulty and loss, it is appropriate to be sad. When sorrow arises, go with it. Observe it. Pay attention to what it is like to experience loss. This recognition of emotions arising was tremendously freeing for me. There were days when I would just realize that I was sad. Sometimes it would just pop into my mind, "Oh, today I am feeling sorrow." It did not mean that it would last all day, or that it would be debilitating. In fact, once recognized, the feeling became my companion and not my master. I was able to go about my business. I set my expectations for myself based on the fact that sadness was going to spend part of the day by my side.

Hello, Come Sit with Me

Mary Stancavage has an expression that really hit home with me, and I think you will find it useful too, ". . . a steady deep intimacy with our experience without preference." She finds that while on retreat, her mind slows down, the chatter goes away, and she is able to make space for something deeper. That is when some of her deepest and perhaps previously unrecognized emotions come to the surface. The first sign of their arrival is often a feeling in her chest or belly. She has learned to give those emotions a silent greeting, "Oh, hello. Come on up. Join me in my practice of insight."

In this way, she tended to the grief that she suppressed over the death of her father. As a child, she did not have the coping skills to express this grief, nor was she encouraged to do anything other than to just move on. The grief was there, waiting for her. She learned to greet it gently. Not to resist it, nor think of it as bad or inconvenient. Just to hold it, watch it, and feel it with kindness and compassion. There was nothing to do about it but just let it be. What a powerful reminder that when something shows up for you in meditation, it is not necessarily a call to action. It is a call to being. Mary reminds us that mindfulness is not just paying attention, it can also be interpreted as being with something. Once you notice your emotion, greet it, and allow it to just be, you might find yourself moving on. "OK grief, that's you. Oh, I am hungry, now grief is replaced with hunger." It is all part of the rising and falling.

In reading this book of shared experiences, with an eye for helping you to understand navigating grief, I am asking you to surrender your expectations. At least in terms of trying to define what you should feel and when you should feel it. Now I understand why some of our wise teachers were hesitant to describe grief. You will need to have your own experience. It's like that warning label you read on personal care products or medications. Potential results and side effects are listed, along with "your results may vary." I think it is fair to say here that your results will vary.

But do not stop reading. Remember the goal is for you to gain insight into how other Buddhists have walked this path. And on this path, many emotions will rise up to meet you. It is very likely that joy and sadness will be two of your visitors. They might even arrive together. Remember, accepting what you view as positive and accepting what you view as negative are critical parts of your practice. Cherry-picking what you will or will not feel is not the way forward.

Chapter 12

Don't Let Fear Stop You

It is important to remember that it is OK to need help—to need community. You need people to help you in the bereavement process, and to work with you as you become death ready. Remember that community is an important part of your practice. The Buddha did not intend for his followers to walk alone. That is why he taught the importance of the Triple Gems.

1. Take refuge in the Buddha
2. Take refuge in the Dhamma
3. Take refuge in the Sangha—find a reputable Buddhist group and become part of the community. You are not meant to practice on your own.

If you want to help someone who is navigating death, one of the best things you can do is let them know that they are not alone. If you are able to step in and be there for them, that is a tremendous gift. Many people have an extreme fear of death and dying and difficult emotions, and this prevents them from really being available. Others are afraid that they will do or say the wrong thing. You know what? You might. But if your intention is pure, and you are offering loving support, you are less likely to do so. If your reason for being with someone is truly about helping that person, you will not say things that make you feel better. In hindsight, I can share with you that *most* of the time, I was happy to have the support of my friends who were able to spend time with me, even when they said things that were misguided. The only thing that was more helpful? The friends who understood that they were not required to say anything, that simply sitting with me was enough.

Develop a Mind Filled with Compassion

If you cannot be there for someone physically or via technology, you can still send loving kindness and compassion. You can dedicate your meditation. Wishing that someone will be well, happy, at ease, and free from suffering is acting. There is an important symbiosis between dwelling in compassion and acting compassionately.

In his book, *Compassion in the Āgamas and Nikāyas*, Bhikkhu Anālayo reminds us,

> *"The meditative cultivation of compassion and compassionate activity through teaching and a secluded lifestyle reinforce each other. Both are integral parts of a dynamic circle of compassion which benefits both oneself and others."*

If you are unable to spend time with someone who is grieving, or with someone who is terminally ill, you can engage in sending loving kindness and compassion through your meditation. You can take on the contemplative role. This is beneficial for both of you.

> *If, with a mind free from hate,*
> *one arouses love toward just one being,*
> *one thereby becomes good.*
> *Compassionate in mind toward all beings,*

> *the noble one generates abundant merit.*
> *(AN 8.1)*

With consistent practice, your contemplative compassion for others is likely to give you the encouragement you need to one day be able to overcome your fear and be with the grieving or dying.

Be honest with yourself. A friend of mine once reminded me of all the support that she had given to me after two of my family members died. I did not have the same recollection. I do not recall seeing her or hearing from her for months. I expressed surprise that our memories were so different. She paused and said, "Oh, well, but you were on my mind constantly, and I was so upset and depressed because of what you had to go through." My experience triggered severe emotional upset for her. This is not the same as offering me support. There is no shame in this, no blame to be assigned. If you find that someone else's difficult situation brings you challenges, this is an opportunity for growth and learning—to get yourself the support you need. You can start with contemplating on compassion for yourself, and when the time comes that you are no longer triggered by death and grief, turn your compassion toward others.

Give the Gift of Peace

Sometimes people are so opposed to death that they seem to support life at all costs. There are times when death is really a positive step. Seth Segall saw this when his wife was in her final stages of cancer. She was suffering, and when she died, it was a peaceful release.

Some people either do not believe in that peaceful release or they believe that death is something to be delayed, to be held at bay for as long as possible.

With his cancer, my husband had reached a point where he was never going to be well. He was in pain and in and out of consciousness. I recall explaining this to a friend. My friend kept insisting that I must have wanted my husband to be alive for as long as possible. It became clear to me that for this friend, there was no other appropriate possibility. I was not going to be able to explain to him that death was a release. Rather than have this friend misinterpret me, and think that I wanted my husband to die, I simply stopped the conversation. There is a big difference between maliciously wishing someone dead and understanding when it is time for someone to leave and wishing them a peaceful transition.

The truth is that your fear of death is less likely to be around what you think will happen to your loved one on the other side, and more about your regrets and your worries about living a life without him or her. I know when my husband was dying, I was not worried about where he would go. He was a good man, so he was going to have a good rebirth. I had to face that I had attachment issues. I was afraid of what my new life would be like. When I was sad, it was never over where he had gone, it was all about the fact that I missed him, and I missed the life we had lived together.

One of the challenges with allowing your fear of death into the room where someone is dying is that it can make it difficult to leave this realm peacefully. If you are saying, "Come on, fight harder, you are strong, you can beat this," you risk bringing up guilt or feelings of unworthiness for the dying. There is a time to let go, and to give permission and encouragement to embrace the process of moving on—not to cling and wail "You can't leave me!" The best gift that you can give to the dying is peace—to allow them to be free of agitation in their final moments. The state in which they die directly impacts the quality of their rebirth. A peaceful death and a well-lived life result in a more favorable rebirth.

"The only thing I know for certain is that I don't know anything for certain." This is the perspective that Timber Hawkeye shared with me in terms of his expectations around what death may or may not be like. In the past, when his friends would hold AIDS death parties, and he knew that he would not see them again, rather than admit they were dead, he would pretend that they had moved to Europe. Now he accepts that the reality is much greater than a trip to a Europe. They went into the unknown—on the ultimate adventure that eventually we will all experience. Beyond that, Timber does not feel the need to spend time contemplating what it will be like.

Proceed with Curiosity

Timber doesn't like to research a hiking trail—he likes to go on the hike and have the experience of the hike without preconceived notions. Since nobody can really tell us about rebirth, or life after death, why not go on that journey with the same enthusiasm as he does for a new hiking trail?

"When the day comes, I'm going to go on that journey with the same enthusiasm. I went on a backpacking trip across New Zealand. You know, it was just like, let's see what unfolds. If you live your life thinking, oh my gosh, what if it's horrible? What if it's bad? What if I don't want to go? Should I look it up? Should I look at the possibility of the hiking trail having snakes on it? Oh my God, let it just go and just have the experience. I don't check the weather. And that may be seen as irresponsible by some. And that's why I think it's such an individual experience, and in my experience, life has been such an incredible journey itself, not knowing one day from the next what's going to unfold, no matter how much I try to plan, no matter how much I tried to look ahead. And no matter how many reviews someone leaves about a trail their experience is going to be different from mine. So, I don't give it any weight. I take it all with a big grain of salt. If I take it at all. And just proceed with curiosity, not caution."

Yes please, let's proceed with curiosity, not caution! How can you and I accomplish this? Venerable Sumitta reminds us to get back to the basics and to be consistent in our practice. Meditating daily will refresh your feelings of inner peace. It will help with your family life and your work life. A regular meditation practice helps keep you balanced. He also emphasized the value of keeping your heart and your mind open to death. Death will come, you do not need to worry about it, but you would be unwise to ignore it. If you hide away from death, when it is time to face it, you will be in real trouble. You will panic. With a strong practice, you can face death with confidence. Embrace impermanence, understand the causes of suffering, and you will develop more peace. Let go of any regret you have over your past actions. None of us is perfect. A clear and peaceful mind is strong and ready to move forward with equanimity.

No, You Stop!

Venerable Sumitta reminds us all, "If Aṅgulimāla can do it, so can you." Aṅgulimāla was a thief and a murderer. During the time of the Buddha, he wandered the countryside stealing whatever he desired, and killing as the mood struck him. His name comes from the garland (mala) he wore around his neck. That garland was made of fingers (anguli)—one finger from each of his victims. One day, he set his sights on killing the Buddha. As the story goes, no matter how fast he ran, Aṅgulimāla was unable to catch up with the Buddha. The Buddha was simply walking, but he was uncatchable. Aṅgulimāla called out for him to stop, to which the Buddha replied:

> *"I have stopped, Aṅgulimāla,*
> *once and for all,*
> *having cast off violence*
> *toward all living beings.*
> *You, though,*

> *are unrestrained toward beings.*
> *That's how I've stopped*
> *and you haven't."*
> *[Aṅgulimāla:]*
> *"At long last a greatly revered great seer*
> *for my sake*
> *has come to the great forest.*
> *Having heard your verse*
> *in line with the Dhamma,*
> *I will go about*
> *having abandoned evil."*
> *So saying, the bandit*
> *hurled his sword and weapons*
> *over a cliff*
> *into a chasm,*
> *a pit.*
> *Then the bandit paid homage*
> *to the feet of the One Well-gone,*
> *and right there requested the Going-forth.*
> *The Awakened One,*
> *the compassionate great seer,*
> *the teacher of the world, along with its devas,*
> *said to him then:*
> *"Come, bhikkhu."*
> *That in itself*
> *was bhikkhuhood for him. (MN 86)*

Venerable Sumitta is right: we can decide to stop—stop engaging in behavior that leads to suffering, and start creating the kind of practice that will allow us to overcome our fear of death.

Suffering to End Suffering

Something that Dave Smith said captured my attention:

"If you put all the religions on a world stage, Buddhism is the most uncomfortable character on that stage because religion essentially is about consolation. Yes, you're going to die. But it's okay because this is going to happen or what religions typically do is they console your deepest fears about life. Buddhism is not interested in that at all. Buddhism is like, this is how it is. And you can develop practices and you can develop strategies and lots of Buddhist ideas and frameworks and concepts, but ultimately, it's all about an acceptance towards that which is most painful."

If you are interested in Buddhism because you will not have to experience suffering, Dave will tell you that you have it backward. His belief is that Buddhism is about learning to live with suffering. This passage from the Pāli Canon takes it further—you live with suffering, and the goal is to become free from suffering.

> *And how is liberation its core? Here, the teachings have been taught by me to my disciples for the utterly complete destruction of suffering. Through liberation one experiences those teaching in just the way that I have taught them to my disciples for the utterly complete destruction of suffering. It is in this way that liberation is its core. (AN IV 245:3)*

There is no magic Buddhist smoothie that you can drink every morning to end suffering. You have to do the work. In order to go beyond suffering, you need to go through the suffering, and really become one with an understanding of the source of your suffering. Your Buddhist practice is what will guide you on the path. One of the ways I think of it is that the Buddha was an amazing teacher. He spent forty years teaching the way to alleviate suffering. He was able to reach different audiences in different ways. He adjusted the complexity of his teachings to make the most impact, and to provide the most benefit to those in attendance. It is not that his teachings are difficult to comprehend, it is that they are difficult to put into practice.

Think about it: you know that a regular meditation practice is to your own benefit. Now think of the many reasons you use to avoid it, such as "I do not have time," or "I can't sit still," or "It is selfish for me to take this time away from my family," or "I don't know how." Part of what you might not be saying out loud is that sitting with your thoughts is difficult. When it is just you and your mind sitting on the cushion, difficult memories surface, unpleasant sensations rise, and your emotions run amok. In comparison, Ebenezer Scrooge in *A Christmas Carol* had it easy. He only had to deal with three ghosts over the course of one night. He dealt with his past, his present, and his future.

The real suffering comes from reliving the same painful experiences over and over again. Your practice will not make your traumatic childhood go away. Your practice will not give everyone you love eternal life. You will still have the same experiences, but now you can drop the adjective—no more painful experiences, just experiences. That is what your consistent practice will bring to you. A human rebirth is a rare gift, so use it well.

> *Staying at Savatthi. Then the Blessed One, picking up a little bit of dust with the tip of his fingernail, said to the monks, "What do you think, monks? Which is greater: the little bit of dust I have picked up with the tip of my fingernail, or the great earth?*
>
> *"The great earth is far greater, lord. The little bit of dust the Blessed One has picked up with the tip of his fingernail is next to nothing. It doesn't even count. It's no comparison. It's not even a*

> *fraction, this little bit of dust the Blessed One has picked up with the tip of his fingernail, when compared with the great earth.*
>
> *"In the same way, monks, few are the beings reborn among human beings. Far more are those reborn elsewhere. Thus you should train yourselves: 'We will live heedfully.' That's how you should train yourselves." (SN 20.2)*

It is good to be a human. It is also hard to be a human. And for many of us, conquering our fear of death is our biggest challenge.

Chapter 13

Death Practices

I recall in the early stages of my grief, Cayce Howe came to meditate with me. One of the tools he gave me to combat my grief was Tonglen meditation. The Tibetan meditation practice of taking on the suffering of others, and sending it back out into the world as loving-kindness. He told me that if in this practice I thought of the suffering of other widows and took their suffering and transformed that suffering, it would help me too. And he was right. It took my mind off my suffering, and it allowed me to do something helpful.

One of my classmates brought me the book, *The Issue at Hand: Essays on Buddhist Mindfulness Practice*, by Gil Fronsdal. It helped me get back to the basics. For me, returning to the basics meant revisiting the Four Noble Truths.

There is stress and suffering, or *dukkha*. Another way to think of this is that in life, we have much dissatisfaction.

We experience this dissatisfaction because we become attached to either wanting good things to stay the same, or for difficult things to stop being difficult.

There is a way out of this dissatisfaction.

The way out of this dissatisfaction is to live your life in accordance with the Noble Eightfold Path.

As I observed my experiences, I fully accepted the truth of dissatisfaction. You cannot fully embrace impermanence without embracing death. The way to embrace death is not to ignore it or deny it, but to make it part of your life, and understand that it is your karma that determines what will happen to you. Your karma is made up of your past actions and your current actions. Nobody can tell you exactly what will happen to you and when it will happen.

Developing an understanding of suffering, karma, and impermanence allowed me to accept death.

In Theravāda Buddhism, *maraṇasati*, or mindfulness of death practices, exists to help practitioners face death with a peaceful mind. These practices come from primary teachings that focus on realizing that death will come, and that it can come at any moment. This realization, when properly contemplated, removes fear and leads to greater insight into the true nature of the dhamma (dharma).

> *When a noble disciple has thus understood aging and death, the origin of aging and death, the cessation of aging and death, and the way leading to the cessation of aging and death . . . he here and now makes an end of suffering. In that way too a noble disciple is one of right view . . . and has arrived at this true Dhamma.*
> (MN 9.23)

If you are a Tibetan Buddhist, consider reading *The Tibetan Book of the Dead* by Padmasambhava, or *The Tibetan Book of Living and Dying* by Sogyal Rinpoche. You might be drawn to the work of Roshi Joan Halifax, or to the writings of Thich Nhat Hanh. We live in an age where we have the good fortune to have access to different schools of Buddhism, different teachers, and different traditions. If you practice within a specific school, there is nothing wrong with seeking out resources from other schools, but keep in mind that for most of us, the way to truly deepen your practice is through consistency—that means practicing on a regular basis and within the same Buddhist school.

At a high level, what these practices give you is the ability to confront your loss, acknowledge your grief, and accept the reality of impermanence. Your meditation and chanting and other devotional practices also help your deceased loved one have a better rebirth.

Your own family probably has some rituals and traditions around death. These might be unique to your family, or part of your cultural and religious tradition. My father died two days before Thanksgiving. What this meant was that some of the resources we needed were taking time off to enjoy the holiday. It took more time than usual to receive an official cause of death, for the cremation to be approved and scheduled, and to receive death certificates. There was the matter of scheduling the funeral services with the church. My mother would absolutely *not* commit to any date for a funeral until she knew when he would be cremated. At first, this was very challenging to me. I heard her priest give her some dates for the funeral, but Mom would not commit. Between traveling from out of state, balancing work, hiring a pet sitter, and booking airfare, I really wanted her to pick a date. And I was dealing with my own grief over losing my father. One of Mom's friends could sense my frustration. She quietly pulled me aside and reminded me that what my mother wanted was a funeral mass. I still was not understanding—I thought that was what I heard the priest trying to arrange. Her friend patiently explained to me that to have the service without my father's ashes meant that it was not a funeral mass, it was a memorial service. Oh! Now the light bulb went on in my head. Of course, a Catholic funeral mass was what my mother wanted my father to have. I was able to let go of all of my needs to plan and move forward more quickly. The most important thing was to work with my mother and to ensure that her needs were met. To follow her rituals and traditions would help ease the pain of her loss, or at least, not make her pain more intense.

Two years later, when Mom and Ed died, I received a taste of my own medicine when one of my friends continued to push her beliefs and traditions on me. She came from a different Buddhist tradition, and her practice was that when someone dies, you are supposed to leave the body undisturbed for two days. This was not something that Ed and I embraced. Since he died at home, the standard procedure was to have a member of the hospice team come verify the death and then call the mortuary. My friend was unable to accept this. She reprimanded me multiple times for what I had done. To make matters even worse, she discussed it with quite a few people. She went to a professor who taught at our school and asked him for advice about what should be done because I had not left my husband's body sit in my house for two days. She was quite vocal about the whole thing. Not only could she not let it go, but when we discussed that my mother had died, she expressed how good it was that my mother died at home alone and was found two days after her death.

Just like my mother and my friend, you probably have some ideas around the right way to handle death, and how to celebrate a life. You might know in your heart that your way is the way that will guarantee a peaceful death and a good rebirth, or best of all, no rebirth. Before you push forward, remember that across the Buddhist traditions there are different beliefs around how to handle death, and how and when rebirth occurs. There are cultural and familial traditions, and many of these are about taking care of the living. Please proceed with compassion.

Find Your Balance

When we spoke, Holly Hisamoto was working for a hospice. Death was part of her daily life. She found that as important as practicing death is, it is also essential to balance her exposure to death with a healthy exposure to life. Some days coming home to her new kitten was a source of light and happiness. A cute, fuzzy baby animal helped to lift some of the heaviness. Because, even with a healthy acceptance of death, there can still be heaviness.

Holly also recommends regular meditation—find one in your specific tradition that helps you maintain a balanced relationship with death, or use music to keep yourself grounded or recite a mantra. I remember that just after my mother and husband died, Cayce Howe recommended that I use a mantra. Specifically, the mantra was to help me when I felt overwhelmed about handling the arrangements for both of them, and when the idea of traveling to my mother's house to begin the process of closing out the material aspects of her life seemed like too much. It was a simple mantra, "I am calm, cared for, and connected." It did the trick. Truth be known, I still use it today when I am feeling overwhelmed.

In his hospice work during the AIDS pandemic, Noël Alumit did notice that meditation was a useful coping device for both the hospice team and the patients. Because he was in a multicultural environment, he had the chance to observe some cultural rituals that provided a way to be active with the balance of life and death. For example, capturing and releasing fish as a way of expressing compassion, or burning specific paper goods as a way to release negative energy. He never felt that any of the rituals he observed were strange, because he could see how they brought some type of relief to the participants.

Live in Peace, Die in Peace

For Seth Segall, death awareness is about life. This awareness makes life richer and more poignant—a reminder that every second is precious. It is a motivator. The idea of living with a limited amount of time does not feel wrong to him. He knows that death will come. There are multiple ways in which it could happen, and if he has to decide about a life-prolonging treatment versus a shorter life with less pain and suffering, he is ready. He realizes that for most of us, there are moments we want to witness. A graduation or wedding, or to finish writing a book. He will stay as long as he can. When it is his time to die, something will be left unfinished. That is how it works.

Ultimately, Seth values Buddhism, not as a tool to achieve some ultimate form of perfection, but as something that increases our humanity, and enables us to flourish. And while it enables us to be ready for death, more importantly, Buddhism helps us live a really good life. As he discusses this, he draws on the ideas of Aristotle and *Utopia*—the idea of living a life that is mostly happy, and that in this life, you are mostly good, meaning that you are truthful, kind, and compassionate. His preference is for reframing how he thinks of Buddhism—to stop looking at it as a cure for pain, and to start looking at it as a code on how to live an excellent life. If you can do this, when your death comes, you have nothing to fear.

Timber Hawkeye equated the creation of *The Death Dhamma Podcast* and this book as a way of putting us all in a box of mirrors. In the box of mirrors, there is no escaping your reflection. And yes, in having these discussions and speaking and writing about death, I am asking all of us to look at death. To be with it. Because there is no escaping it. Remember that Timber reminds us not to take the attitude of, "I will cross that bridge when I get there." We are *all* already on that bridge.

Death is not something that may or may not happen. There is no reason to worry about it, but if we process it emotionally, spiritually, and mentally, and come to peace, that is when we can become the most alive. His assessment: "In a sense, if we live in peace, then we can die in peace."

There are ways to prepare for your own death. Venerable Karma Lekshe Tsomo taught me that for a person who has done a lot of meditation, it is advantageous to die slowly. This allows you to understand all the different stages of the dissolution of the body and mind. This takes training and years of practice. As we deal with the loss of others, it is a reminder that we can prepare for our end of life. We will lose our identity, and our bodies will fall apart. We have spent our lifetime building our identity and caring for our body, only to have to let go of it all.

Because she experienced great pain and near death from a snakebite, she knows that in your final moments, your mind can be clouded with medication and pain. This makes it even more important to engage in death and dying practices in advance. You do not know what you will be up against until you train.

Death is what brought Venerable Karma Lekshe Tsomo to Buddhism. After her beloved dog Scampi and some family members died, she was never satisfied with the answers she received about what happened, or why it had happened. She came across a book on Zen. In a "there are no coincidences in life" scenario, her family name was Zenn. Of course she had to investigate. She read the *Way of Zen* by Alan Watts, and *Zen Buddhism* by D. T. Suzuki. She recalls reading the books from cover to cover and knowing that she had found something that made complete sense to her. This was in the 1950s, and information about Buddhism was not available like it is today. She scoured every bookshop she encountered.

As she looked more deeply into Buddhism, she learned about a whole system of understanding death, life, and rebirth.

She recounts, ". . . that made a lot of sense to me because the idea that we die, and we just disappear into nothingness doesn't make a lot of sense to me. I mean, the material body, of course, decomposes. But what about the consciousness, where does it go? You know, and the idea of going to heaven. It was too abstract, the rebirth theory made a lot more sense to me at that time, and even also the whole idea of karma, cause and effect, and how it continues over lifetimes. To me, this idea is much more reasonable."

A little bit later, and in another part of Southern California, I would develop similar beliefs. I didn't understand or come across Buddhism until much later in my life. When I did, it was like, "Oh, it is like this." It was just something that made sense to me.

Strength Training Requires Strong Teaching

Death practice is serious business. It is difficult. It requires mental, emotional, and spiritual strength. Most of us cannot just dive right in and do a charnel ground meditation. It is not surprising that many people seek to avoid dealing with death until it is absolutely necessary. And it makes sense that those who faced death very early and without tools turned to denial and numbing themselves. You need to have a trusted guide. Dave Smith found a dharma teacher in Stephen Smith. I think it is best to let Dave tell the story:

"We spend the night at what's now the Barre Center for Buddhist Studies and then in the morning a dharma teacher named Stephen Smith, who I'm still very close with today, came over, and he sat down with me. It was six o'clock in the morning and still dark out. And he said, 'Tell me about your experience' and I went on to tell him about my sister and I just kind of gave him the litany of my autobiographical suffering. For some reason I trusted this guy. No reason why, I really just trusted this guy. And we had this long conversation about the First Noble Truth about dukkha, or suffering. He reframed my experience in a very interesting way where he said, 'Actually, there's a lot of wisdom that you have now because your heart has been ripped open and you actually are experiencing suffering on a very real level, like this is how it is. This is the truth. And you've gotten a very, very poignant specific sense of that. Now the question is, what do you want to do about that?'"

He introduced Dave to mindfulness meditation, and Dave recalls knowing that something had happened that day—that part of him came back online, back into being aware of his choices. Stephen Smith was the first adult to tell Dave the truth. He did not chastise him for his feelings or actions. He just sat down with him and validated his experience. That is what a trusted teacher can do.

When Diane Wilde could not sit in meditation, and she thought that she was not being a good enough Buddhist, her teacher listened to her and told her to try walking meditation. Because in her early stages of grief, she needed to move, and to feel the grief in her body. Her teacher did not shame her or tell her to just keep sitting. He helped her find a way to experience her suffering in a way that would be beneficial to her. That is also what a trusted teacher can do. Please be careful and thoughtful with yourself, and with your practice. We are not meant to practice alone. The Buddha traveled with an entire community of monks. You need a community too.

No matter what death practices you use, you would be wise to keep these thoughts from Venerable Karma Lekshe Tsomo in mind. "Well, I think the most important thing is to recognize that the way we live our lives will set the stage for how we die. If we live a life of kindness, compassion, doing our best to achieve wisdom. If we do wholesome actions and try to avoid unwholesome actions. In other words, living an ethical life, then

I think that our future, some of it will shape up nicely for us. You know, because everything depends on causes and conditions, but the overall view is that if we live an ethical, compassionate life, really our future is assured, we don't have to worry about it."

Chapter 14

How to Help Yourself

Perhaps one of the best ways to help yourself become comfortable with death and grief is to recognize that you are *not* comfortable with death and grief. Do you know what that means? You are normal! Holly Hisamoto just came right out and said it, "I think that it has been helpful for me to just normalize that it's OK to be afraid. It's OK to be anxious, that will come up. You can survive that feeling, try it anyway. And then also recognize that death can be awkward." Yes, exactly. As she discussed that we can be fearful and uncomfortable, she also mentioned the importance of understanding how we deal with loss in general, because the way in which you act when you lose your credit card can help you to understand the way in which you will cope with a more significant loss. Any kind of loss is a form of letting go and can be used as practice for our finale, our ultimate letting go.

Be Your Own Best Friend

As Noël Alumit says, "Practice radical self-compassion for yourself. The whole idea is, don't think that you're doing anything wrong. Oh, I should get up sooner. Oh, I should be exercising. Look, you are doing the very best you can."

He recalls a time during the AIDS pandemic when he and his co-volunteers were chastised for spending time assembling safer-sex kits. They spent hours putting them together. Their director told them that they should be spending their time differently, and that others should be putting together the kits. The staff therapist stepped in and advised the director that what they were doing was good for their mental health. They were together and having this communal experience of doing something proactive. The repetitive nature of the task helped them process the grief and trauma that they were experiencing. It was during this time that a wise woman reminded Noël that it was time to slow down, and to not worry about productivity. Very insightfully she said, "We are human beings, not human doings."

When Noël repeated this phrase to me, he thought that I must have heard it before, but I had not. And what an amazing reminder for all of us. When you are going through grief, it is OK to *be* and to not to worry about how much you *do*. You will *do* once you give yourself time to *be*. This is definitely in agreement with what Mary Stancavage taught me. Just because something comes up for you in meditation does not mean it is a call to action. It might be a call to being.

As you feel grief or fear of death, think about how you are expressing yourself, whether through your internal dialog, or in communications with others. You could be unintentionally creating a lasting narrative. Here is an example of a narrative from a man who carried guilt and trauma over a divorce: "Twenty years ago I went through this horrible, painful traumatic divorce. It just tore our family apart." Upon hearing this narrative, Timber Hawkeye asked the man if he could say it again, but this time dropping all the adjectives. The man thought about it and said, "Twenty years ago I went through a divorce." When he dropped the adjectives, he also dropped the weight of the judgment he was carrying around due to the divorce. Practice dropping the adjectives from your statements around your loss—it can help you come to a place of acceptance.

Gratitude and Acceptance

When Mary Stancavage needs an immediate way to intercept painful emotions, she uses this mantra: "Right now it is like this." Her mantra helps her pause and consider what is happening right now, in her body and in her mind, and accept that whatever she is feeling right now is OK. It keeps her from being overrun by her thoughts and fears.

As you come to a place where you can accept how things are, allow your gratitude practice to kick in. What is it that you can appreciate? I remember trying to figure out the benefits of having the two people who were closest to me die within one week of each other. It came to me as people asked how I was doing, and I would reply, "I am as well positioned as possible for such a difficult situation."

It was true. I had a roof over my head. I had food on the table. I did have other people who cared about me. I had some degree of security and did not have to make big life-changing decisions. I lived by the beach with a path perfect for contemplative walks. I had two crazy cats who knew to stay close to me. I had a friend who brought me giant croissants. I had another friend who went with me to my mother's out-of-state funeral. I had an uncle who called me every Sunday morning (before the Patriots game) to check on me.

The more I looked for things to be grateful for, the more I found. Each day, I challenged myself to come up with three things for which I was grateful. Some days were more difficult than others, but it was possible to find three things every day, even if on some days I needed to repeat a list from a previous day.

Did I mention that I had two crazy cats? While cats do not receive high marks for being caring or empathetic, my two definitely rallied around me. One of them was always right next to me. Sometimes I wondered if perhaps they had set up some type of schedule. One had mornings, the other had afternoons, and they both took evenings. At night when I was trying to sleep, one or both of them would curl up right next to me. Maybe it was because there was extra room in the bed, or maybe it was cold, but I knew that I was not alone. The healing power of having a pet to take care of cannot be overemphasized.

While I never felt suicidal, I certainly experienced depression. Having two furry creatures depending on me for their care was a great way to help take me out of myself. For a few moments each day, my thoughts were directed toward their care. One of them had been especially close to Ed, and I did worry about how she would handle his death. She became my "watch cat." It seemed like every time I turned around, there she was, keeping an eye on me. Taking care of the cats gave me some purpose. Something to do beyond feeling sad or attending to the business of death. On days when I did not want to be around humans, I had companionship. When I talked to myself (yes, I did that), at least there was another creature within earshot. Cats are definitely a good reminder that you are not the center of the universe. The healing power of our pets is amazing. Not your entire salvation, but another area to help you through your difficult time.

Back to the Basics

When I was in a period of deep grieving, returning to the basics of my Buddhist practice was truly helpful. When we were discussing helpful teachings, one of the first things that Venerable De Hong said was to go back to the Four Noble Truths. Pay attention to the First Noble Truth, and you will read:

> *Now this, monks, is the noble truth of stress:*
> *Birth is stressful, aging is stressful,* ***death is***
> ***stressful; sorrow, lamentation, pain,***
> ***distress, and despair*** *are stressful;*
> *association with the unbeloved is stressful,*
> *separation from the loved is stressful, not*
> *getting what is wanted is stressful. In short, the*
> *five clinging-aggregates are stressful. (SN 56.11)*

Venerable De pointed out that death is a physical process that brings psychological and emotional suffering. When the dead are at peace, it is the survivors who will experience the *dukkha*. In addition to the First Noble Truth, Venerable De reminded me about the Five Recollections. We discussed these in the section on Training for Death. Remember, "I am of the nature to die." Since he is ordained in both the Theravāda and the Mahāyāna traditions, Venerable De knows that the recollections are chanted or read daily by Buddhist monks and nuns around the globe. As laypeople, we too can access the recollections—to really recognize that we will die, and to remember to pay attention to our loved ones and to what is going on around us right now. There is balance for us to achieve between taking care of others and taking care of ourselves. The stronger we are mentally, emotionally, physically, and spiritually, the more that we can be of service to ourselves and our loved ones.

Each year on his birthday, Venerable De reminds us that he is one year closer to the casket. He is not being dismissive of the many birthday greetings he receives. He is reminding us that aging is part of our experience. If you are fortunate to age, you are recognizing the signs of death. This is not pessimism, it is realism.

For Venerable Guan Zhen, the teachings on Dependent Origination (*Pratītyasamutpāda*) helped him through his grief. At a high level, these teachings help us grasp that when one condition exists, other conditions will arise. For example, the fact that you are born means that you will die. Or, using the First Noble Truth, when desire arises, suffering will arise. When there is clinging and attachment, there will also be suffering. A brief overview of this teaching:

> *When this exists, that comes to be. With the arising of this, that arises. When this does not exist, that does not come to be. With the cessation of this, that ceases. (SN 12.61)*

This excerpt provides a more elaborative discussion, and I am including it here to provide additional context—it is *not* the full teaching.

> *If one is asked, "Is there a demonstrable requisite condition for aging and death?" one should answer, "There is."*
>
> *If one is asked, "From what requisite condition do aging and death come?" one should say, "Aging and death come from birth as their requisite condition."*
>
> *If one is asked, "Is there a demonstrable requisite condition for birth?" one should answer, "There is."*
>
> *If one is asked, "From what requisite condition does birth come?" one should say, "Birth comes from becoming as its requisite condition."*
>
> *If one is asked, "Is there a demonstrable requisite condition for becoming?" one should answer, "There is."*
>
> *If one is asked, "From what requisite condition does becoming come?" one should say,*

> *"Becoming comes from clinging as its requisite condition." (DN 15)*

This is a good place to point out that, while *most* Buddhist schools agree on the Four Noble Truths, the Noble Eightfold Path, and Dependent Origination, when we get into the details of the teachings, they are not all exactly the same. Venerable Guan Zhen is a Buddhist monk who is advanced on his path, and in his understanding of the teaching, has a much deeper understanding than I have. I can see the value of the teachings, and why they are useful in coming to terms with death and grief. These are teachings that really help integrate the truth of suffering, and our role in our own suffering.

Contemplating Death

Diane Wilde has drawn on *maraṇasati*, or mindfulness of death practices for several years. There are two primary mindfulness of death suttas in the Pāli Canon. In the first, *Aṅguttara Nikāya (AN) 6.19*, the focus is on the right way to develop mindfulness of death. You really need to understand the difference between thinking that you will live long enough to finish your meal versus understanding you could die while chewing one bite of that same meal. In the second, AN 6.20, the Buddha encourages his monks to contemplate the many ways in which death can come. Contemplate this during the day, and contemplate this as day turns to night, and as night turns into day. By following these two teachings, you will cultivate mindfulness of death.

Mary Stancavage mentioned a similar type of teaching from Tibetan Buddhism, specifically, the teachings of Atisha, and his contemplations on death.

1. Death is inevitable.
2. Our life span is decreasing continuously.
3. Death will come, whether or not we are prepared for it.

4. Human life expectancy is uncertain.
5. There are many causes of death.
6. The human body is fragile and vulnerable.
7. At the time of death, our material resources are not of use to us.
8. Our loved ones cannot keep us from death.
9. Our own body cannot help us at the time of our death.

I cannot place enough emphasis on the need for us to fully accept death as part of our human experience. And the path to this acceptance is to contemplate on it, and to include death as part of your practice.

Each of the Buddhist schools approaches the topic of death and impermanence in their own way. There is overlap, but flitting around from one school to another might be confusing. Returning to the idea of training, you will experience more growth when you work with a consistent and focused plan.

Consistency Is Key

Our twelve wise teachers come from different Buddhist schools, and perhaps one of our teachers might identify as being more secular, or spiritual with Buddhist leanings. Through them, you and I have had the collective benefit of years of experience, wisdom, and practice. I would not expect you to follow everything that has been shared with you. For many of us, the most helpful approach is to be consistent in our paths. This does not mean that you cannot read both the *Tibetan Book of Living and Dying* and the *Maraṇasati Sutta*. It does mean that in your practice, you will reap the most benefits if you find the Buddhist teachings and teacher who resonant the most with you.

You live in a time where Buddhist teachings are accessible. Each school offers different teachings and different ways for you to invite death into your practice. Work with a teacher. Sit with your community. Practice consistently.

As we wrapped up our discussion, Venerable Sumitta said to me, "Don't regret about the past, just don't daydream about your future. Don't panic about your future too much. Just live in the present moment, be happy, and do good and be good as much as you can. And that is the best way for you to be happy all the time." He was not advocating hedonism—he was reminding me to be consistent in my practice. "When you do, for example, a certain meditation, even during your last breath, you will be aware of it. You know, this is my last minute, you know that much peace comes to you when you practice meditation."

Practice consistently and faithfully, and in death you can remain calm. You will have a peaceful death, which leads to a more favorable rebirth. Remember the wise practice ardently—now is the time.

Chapter 15

Death Dhamma Ahas

Having access to so much collective experience and wisdom led me to wonder, was there anything about death or grief that surprised our wise teachers? I asked, and from this question came some very interesting stories and perspectives for us to consider as we continue our death training.

Other Cultures Can Teach You About Death

When you visit other countries for an extended visit, you will have the opportunity to see how people in different cultures deal with death. Venerable Karma Lekshe Tsomo observed, "You know where we all live as part of a larger community. We're all born into a family of some description and all of these things influence the way that we understand and way that we handle death. So there's tremendous variety, even within the Buddhist world. What I found is that people are aware of the teaching that death is definite, but the time of death's indefinite." She saw firsthand how those who understood this teaching were very well prepared to handle death and dying.

Once, while staying at a monastery in northeastern Thailand, Venerable Karma Lekshe Tsomo attended a funeral for a young man who had died in a motorcycle accident. He had dedicated much of his time to helping the nuns at the monastery. He was an only child, and his parents were grief-stricken. Yet they handled the loss of their son with dignity and wisdom. Of course they were sad, but their understanding of death and impermanence helped them cope with their loss. She relayed to me, "I was so impressed. You know people can have PhDs or, you know, millions of attainments and yet not understand these basic life skills, how to deal with the tragedies, the inevitable misfortunes of life. So for this simple peasant family to be able to process this calmly and compassionately, it was so beautiful to see."

There is a lot to be said for the type of wisdom we can obtain if we move from knowing something academically or intellectually versus knowing something in our hearts. This family knew Buddhism in their hearts. What Venerable Karma Lekshe Tsomo saw was that these parents understood that their son had lived a good life. He was helping the monastery. He was creating wholesome actions every day. So even though they were mourning, they could also take solace in understanding that their son had lived a very good life. She further explained to me:

"By helping the nuns and so on, that, you know, someone could live for one hundred years but not have that kind of good fortune. And in addition, because of his strong connection with the monastery, all of the nuns were immediately ready to say prayers for him the very same day. So, they could give them a very good send off and they believe that by sending good thoughts to the person, it will help their wholesome karma to ripen. In order to achieve a wholesome, you know, fortunate rebirth. So, in a way, although it was a tragedy from one perspective, from another point of view, he was actually in one of the most fortunate circumstances in terms of having a good death."

This is what we are meant to do. No matter what Buddhist school resonates for you.

Buddhism is not just about reciting passages and memorization. Yes, in this book, I draw on the Pāli Canon and use passages to illustrate key points. But in my practice, I seek to not just know a passage and be able to quote it, I am working on internalizing the words into my thoughts and actions. To take the teachings and gain the kind of insight that these parents possessed. I ask you to consider a similar approach. When you decide to memorize a list, mantra, or teaching, please do it because you want to live it. You want it to inform your life and guide your decisions. We have been given teachings and meditation. They are meant to be integrated. We do not just read and memorize; we do not just meditate.

Each Death Reveals Something New

When Venerable Sumitta was a child, his father died. As an adult, and after being a monk for several years, his mother died. Something that surfaced for him after his mother died was an awareness of his father. He began to feel a relationship with his deceased father. He began to understand that his mother did such an amazing job parenting him and his brothers and sisters, that in many ways, they did not feel the hole that was created when his father died. His mother balanced their family dynamic in such a way that they never really felt like they were missing out. When she died, all of a sudden it was like losing both his mother and his father. It was so difficult.

He had been away from his familial home for years. As a monk, he works for the community. The way he described it to me was that all of society is his family. Wherever he goes, he considers the people he stays with to be his family. Despite this definition of family, he still felt a stronger attachment to his mother. And of course, this attachment came up for him as he grieved her loss. It taught him his limitations. It led him to consider rebirth, perhaps she was his mother in past lives, and perhaps she will be his mother again, and he may have had other mothers in other lives. In each case, death comes. Now that she is gone, he dedicates merit to benefit her as she continues on.

Each death that we experience brings us a new lesson. For Venerable Sumitta, losing his mother brought him to a different understanding of the death of his father. His example showed me that all of us have different levels of attachment to different people. When a person dies, that death might actually illuminate something that was lurking in our subconscious. The feelings you expect to arise, or the experience you are expecting might not materialize. Something else will show up instead—another great reminder to be open.

Death Can Be Joyful

The actual process of death is not necessarily heavy and sad. There can be many light moments. The last thing that Diane Wilde's husband did was make her laugh. He was the comedian of the emergency room—so much so, that it made it difficult for the staff to honor his wishes regarding resuscitation. The doctors and nurses were enchanted by him. He used his final well of energy to make others around him happy.

Holly Hisamoto was also able to relay some stories where death was not sad, depressing, or traumatizing. She has seen instances where it was joyful. The environment and the attitudes of the dying and their friends and family shape the experience. She has seen deaths that had the joyful quality of a life well lived, and now ending on a positive note. In her role as a hospice chaplain, she has seen families who are calm and relaxed. Everyone is in the room together, the kids might be playing on the floor, the family dog is there, someone is on the phone, and in the midst of all this, grandma takes one last peaceful breath. Everyone sees that she is gone, and they hug and join together in prayer. Holly has also seen joking and levity. She has been a witness to diversity and beauty in the experience of death.

As an example, she told the story of a woman who was over one hundred years old. She knew that she was in her final days. Her goal was to live long enough for the one hundredth anniversary of the 19th Amendment (Women's Right to Vote). And she made it. She had close relationships with so many of her female relatives. Her daughters, granddaughters, and great-granddaughter were not able to visit in person. So Holly arranged for them to visit her virtually. She had multiple laptops in the room and one of her daughters was on one while the other daughter was on another. In this situation, technology brought her loved ones into the room with her. They all worked to ensure that they could be together. This was not necessarily a spiritual or religious group—they did not engage in prayer. They sang some favorite songs, had some discussion about politics, and read poetry. The term that came to my mind as Holly described it to me was *death party*. It was a death party—a wonderful gathering. And the next day, the woman died. In a way, she had been present at her own memorial.

Mary Stancavage said, "Don't forget the joy, there is always joy." She referenced James Baraz and his course titled, *Awakening Joy*. She found that his materials helped her see that there was joy, and to be with that joy. On the day of her brother's funeral, she and his wife and others were able to have moments where they would laugh and laugh as they recalled some of his exploits. Initially, it felt strange, but then it felt right. Cultivating joy and gratitude in the midst of discomfort is a way to find equanimity. And the joy can make you stronger. It builds up your reserves for those times when the grief arises.

Mary also recommends the work of Dr. Rick Hanson, specifically, the reminder to let in the good thoughts. It is not wrong to think good thoughts when you are grieving. When a good thought surfaces, stay with it for several seconds. This has a beneficial impact on your brain, and it helps to move your negativity bias. It is not a crime to feel joy, even in the middle of a difficult time—it is a good thing.

You do not have to be afraid to express positive thoughts to others. Unfortunately, if every time you communicate with others, you remind them of what a terrible experience you are having, you will push most of them away. You do not want to be over the top and tell others that everything is great, but you can find some middle ground. Consider the contrast between these two statements:

"I have just decided that my life is about difficulty and sadness, and there is no room for happiness right now. Every day is just another horrible day."

versus

"I am doing the best I can in a difficult situation. It is hard, but I have a roof over my head, food on my table, and good people like you, who care about me."

Both describe the same situation. It is all about being able to find some type of balance. The first statement does not allow for any joy or gratitude, and it seems guaranteed to prolong the difficulties. The second statement combines the struggle with the recognition that there are also blessings. You can welcome the blessings; it does not mean you are being disloyal or disrespectful to your deceased loved ones.

Bringing joy and gratitude on board when you are in the depth of sorrow is not easy. I really appreciate how Venerable Karma Lekshe Tsomo reminded me of why we are in the midst of all of this suffering, "Definitely, it's the attachment that brings the pain, attachment and clinging, and if we look directly at them and understand that our attachment really is causing our suffering, then we can begin to loosen those bonds to replace it with pure love. This is quite different in nature from attachment. In the case of attachment, we're looking for something for ourselves. We want that person in our lives to be with us."

What I understood her to say is that we can use our suffering to help us decrease our suffering. The way to do this is being honest about the role that attachment is playing. If we can replace that clinging and wanting them back with a love and appreciation for the fact that they were ever here at all, we can bring joy into our grieving. We can do this by remembering the special moments we spent with them, their positive qualities, and the good times that we shared. We do not need to let overwhelming sadness erase the fun and the love. We can redirect our attachment.

Grief Brings Gifts

Being with the dying and going through your own cycle of grief is going to change you. It might surprise you to learn that this is a process that can bring you gifts if you are ready to receive them.

Diane Wilde found that her Buddhist practice deepened, and that she became even more diligent. She found that after her husband died, she was really able to meditate and dedicate merit to others in a much more meaningful way. She had this realization that other sentient beings were going to have the same experience—that they too will face death—and this made her spiritual endeavors more poignant. She could feel herself becoming kinder and more compassionate. Now she is more willing to be with people who are suffering or dying or grieving. In fact, she feels it is important to be there for them—to visit people, because sometimes others cannot. There are people who have such a fear of hospitals and illness that they cannot be there for their own loved ones. Diane can sit with another woman whose husband is dying because she's already been through it. She understands that there is nothing for her to do other than to be there. Diane understands that this woman is going to go through a difficult time, but she will come through—she just has to do so on her own schedule.

I watched something similar happen with my mother. My father died when they were both in their eighties. She had seen other women around her lose their husbands. And while my mother was not unkind toward those women, she did sound a bit condescending when she mentioned them. In her social group, I noticed that there was a separation between the women who still had husbands and the widows. I am not projecting here, because there was a day when my mother shared with me that she felt guilty for her past attitude about the widows in her group, and that now she more fully understood how they felt. So my mother, Joannie Meloni, the sometime rebel and activist, reached out to the other widows and created stronger bonds with them and made sure they were included in her social activities. After she died, those women missed her so much. I still get cards from some of them each year, and they always mention how much they miss those outings with my mother.

To accept death into your life is to receive a new motivational coach. Each of our teachers received this motivation at different stages in their life. Noël put into words something that we might consider to be a regular part of maturing and cognizing that our time here is limited. Here is how he expressed it to me:

> "I think, you know, ever since I turned 50, it's also become a state of whether I don't have that much time on Earth . . . And that spurred me to get busy really quickly. You know, so I feel like this period. It's about,

oh, I need to create as much as possible. To write more, paint more, photograph more, you know, so we don't know how much time we have left."

One of the gifts of death is a reminder that the gift of time is not limitless. For me, one of the gifts of death was to write a memoir about making friends with death (*Carpooling with Death: How Living with Death Will Make You Stronger, Wiser and Fearless*), start *The Death Dhamma Podcast*, and to help others make friends with death. I truly felt like showing up and speaking and writing about death was important.

You Can Become a Gift to Others

You will learn to stay away from meaningless phrases. I cringe at some of the things I once thought were comforting to others. Now I understand that many of us think that we need to fill the silence, and that we have to say something that seems upbeat or spiritually deep. After my experience, and speaking to others, I see that it is simply OK to say, "I am sorry." Really, the best thing to do is just be quiet and listen. And if the person you are comforting does not need to talk, then just be quiet and experience the stillness together. A person who knows that he or she cannot fix your grief, and is willing to just be there with you, is one of the greatest treasures you can find. So much so, that I encourage you to become that resource to others. Rare is the person who can just be with death and grief. When was the last time you were able to make a huge impact in someone's life, just by saying nothing? All you have to do is sit right next to a human being who is suffering.

Conclusion

It all started with curiosity. Well, actually, it all started when I realized I needed to make friends with death. Then came the curiosity. I knew about my experiences, and how much I leaned on my Buddhist practice as I grieved the deaths of my family members. But what about others? There is a whole community of Buddhists experiencing life and death every day. How do they do this? How do they handle death? So the quest to find experienced teachers began.

I learned very quickly that if someone was going to speak with me, he or she would agree almost immediately. Either my request resonated, or it did not. And as you know, twelve wise and caring people stepped forward to teach me. My goal has been to share those teachings with you, because if you were drawn to this book, then you, too, are curious about how to best make peace with death. You, too, are open to learning from the wisdom and experience of others.

Isn't it wonderful that these men and women, laypeople and monks and nuns, all said, "This is important, of course I will speak with you."? OK, they did not all utter that exact sentence—come on, that would be weird. But each in their own way did express that our ability to become comfortable with death is a critical component to living a happy life.

Our human experiences are at once similar and yet diverse. There is a kind of logic to this. Death is not always the same, but it always comes. Your grief is not the same for each loss, but there will be loss.

You might be the person who learned about death when your dog died, and then when your grandparents died. Or you might be the person who was thrown into death headfirst—losing a parent, sibling, or classmate when you were just a child.

No matter what your first experience with death was, please consider helping others come to terms with death, especially the young. We have seen how sweeping death under the carpet, and trying to act like everything is normal, leads to repressed grief and unexpressed trauma, both of which will hang around and torture you until you deal with it. If you can acknowledge death in real time, you are better positioned to lead a happy and peaceful life. And as you know, a peaceful life helps you have a peaceful death, which leads to a better rebirth. In turn, this can help you reach your last rebirth.

Monks and nuns are not exempt from the experience and emotions that come with death and grief. Each of the monastics who spoke to me lost loved ones at different points in their lives. As they moved forward with their training, they had more resources to draw on. But not one of them said that it was easy, or that to be a Buddhist meant there would be no more sadness. Each reminded me that we can take control by noticing our clinging and our aversion. We want our loved one back. We don't want to have to be sad. What could be more direct teaching of *dukkha?* More acceptance and less resistance will bring you more peace and less suffering.

We all know that death is inevitable, but there is the intellectual knowing, and the deeper knowing that resides in your heart. That knowing in your heart is what will bring you strength and resilience and peace. Please keep doing the work, and keep an open heart. Fight the temptation to wait and "cross that bridge when I come to it." Remember that, as Timber Hawkeye said, once we are born, we are already on that bridge. Or like the cartoon of the movie theater marquee that Seth Zulho Segall treasures, "Coming soon to a neighborhood near you, old age, sickness, and death."

You will see death in many ways, and each death that you encounter will engender different responses in you. Whatever you feel, whatever arises in you, that's great. Feel it in your body. Notice how it impacts you, and remember that you do not have to become that emotion. You are not the embodiment of sadness—you are both scientist and subject of the most important experiment of your life.

I hope this book has inspired you to use the experiences of others, and your own Buddhist practice, to make friends with death. Create your training plan. Even if you think you are not ready, your consistent practice is preparing you. Meditate and develop insight into the rising and falling of your thoughts and emotions. Study the dharma with a reputable teacher. Sit with a dedicated sangha. Even when you think that your meditations and lessons have nothing to do with facing death, you are developing strength and resilience. You are giving yourself the opportunity to experience equanimity. Start by meeting yourself where you are and work your way forward. Please do this for yourself, and for the benefit of others.

Toward the end of our talk, Venerable Karma Lekshe Tsomo asked me to remember that we can offset the outrageous actions of others by bringing more compassion into the home and out to the world, and to share that compassion with everyone we meet.

"Your actions will have an effect on others around you. When you are kind to others, you create a ripple effect. We live in a time when an email can reach the ends of the earth. Just imagine the power that we have to help one another. Do not think for one moment that you cannot make a difference. Your thoughts make a difference. Your ability to act with kindness every day makes a difference. Even as you sit in your deepest grief, you can make a difference."

Take your own suffering day by day, and each day think about how much wisdom and compassion you can share with the world. Each day, it will be different, but every day you have the ability to help yourself and others.

Keep in touch—join my community and keep up with *The Death Dhamma Podcast* and my continued work by visiting *www.margaretmeloni.com*.

May you be well, may you be happy, may you be at ease, and may you be free from suffering.

Resources

Included here are some of the sources that are either mentioned in this book or are directly related to one of our wise teachers. While not an exhaustive list of all sources and teachings available to you and your Death Dhamma practice, it is a good list to continue your work. May you find them to be helpful in your practice.

Books

A Year to Live: How to Live This Year as If It Were Your Last, Stephen Levine

Becoming Water, Cayce Howe

Being with Dying: Cultivating Compassion and Fearlessness in the Presence of Death, Joan Halifax

Buddhism and Human Flourishing, Seth Zulho Segall

Buddhist Boot Camp, Timber Hawkeye

Carpooling with Death: How Living with Death Will Make You Stronger, Wiser and Fearless, Margaret Meloni

Compassion in the Āgamas and Nikāyas, Bhikkhu Anālayo

Encountering Buddhism: Western Psychology and Buddhist Teachings, Seth Zulho Segall

Faithfully Religionless, Timber Hawkeye

Living Zen: A Practical Guide of a Balanced Existence, Seth Zulho Segall

No Death, No Fear: Comforting Wisdom for Life, Thich Nhat Hanh

Tattoos on the Heart: The Power of Boundless Compassion, Gregory Boyle

The Issue at Hand: Essays on Buddhist Mindfulness Practice, Gil Fronsdal

The Tibetan Book of the Dead, Padmasambhava (edited by John Babcock)

The Tibetan Book of Living and Dying, Sogyal Rinpoche

Courses

Awakening Joy by James Baraz

awakeningjoy.info

A Year to Live

This course is offered by multiple teachers at different Buddhist meditation centers throughout the United States. Your best approach is to use a search engine to find a session being taught near you.

Foundations of Well-Being

www.rickhanson.net/online-courses

Podcasts

Buddhist Boot Camp, hosted by Timber Hawkeye

www.buddhistbootcamp.com/podcast

Dave Smith Dharma, hosted by Dave Smith

www.davesmithdharma.com/1465-2

More Happiness Less Suffering, hosted by Cayce Howe and Dr. Monisha Vasa

www.mhlspodcast.com

The Death Dhamma Podcast, hosted by Margaret Meloni

www.margaretmeloni.com/podcast

Websites– People

Noël Alumit: *noelalumit.com*

Timber Hawkeye: *www.buddhistbootcamp.com*

Venerable De Hong: *engagedbuddhistalliance.org*
engagedbuddhistalliance@gmail.com

Cayce Howe: *www.caycehowe.com*

Margaret Meloni: *www.margaretmeloni.com*

Seth Zulho Segall, PhD: *www.existentialbuddhist.com*

Dave Smith: *www.davesmithdharma.com*

Mary Stancavage: *marystancavage.org*

Venerable Sumitta: *www.dhammausa.org*

Venerable Karma Lekshe Tsomo: *sakyadhita.org*

Diane Wilde: *sactoinsight.org/tag/diane-wilde*

Websites–Teachings

"Lama Zopa Rinpoche's Advice to a Person Who Is Dying"

> *fpmt.org/edu-news/advice/lama-zopa-rinpoches-advice-to-a-person-who-is-dying*

"Recollection—Five Subjects for Frequent Recollection"

> *amaravati.org/audio/recollection-five-subjects-for-frequent-recollection-pali-and-english-page-47*

"Merit: The Buddha's Strategies for Happiness"

> *www.dhammatalks.net/Books15/Thanissaro-Bhikkhu_Merit_v130613.pdf*

"Dependent Origination"

www.buddha101.com/p_origin.htm

"Relating to Suicide from a Buddhist Perspective"

www.andrewholecek.com/suicide-from-a-buddhist-perspective

"What Is Metta Meditation?"

tricycle.org/magazine/metta-practice

About the Author

Margaret Meloni is a businessperson, Buddhist practitioner, and host of *The Death Dhamma Podcast*. She advocates the practice of inviting the awareness of death into your life. She has seen how Buddhism, combined with a healthy respect for the Grim Reaper, has helped her create a life with more peace and less suffering.

Visit Margaret at *www.margaretmeloni.com*.